THE LITTLE GENIUS
SERGIO AGÜERO

MATT AND TOM OLDFIELD

DINO

Published by Dino Books
an imprint of John Blake Publishing Ltd
3 Bramber Court, 2 Bramber Road,
London W14 9PB, England

www.johnblakepublishing.co.uk

www.facebook.com/johnblakebooks ▌f
twitter.com/jblakebooks ▌t

First published in paperback in 2017

ISBN: 978 1 78606 218 5

British Library Cataloguing-in-Publication Data:

A catalogue record for this book is available from the British Library.

Design by www.envydesign.co.uk
Cover illustration by Dan Leydon
Background image: Shutterstock

Printed in Great Britain by CPI Group (UK) Ltd

1 3 5 7 9 10 8 6 4 2

Papers used by John Blake Publishing are natural, recyclable products made from
wood grown in sustainable forests. The manufacturing processes conform to the
environmental regulations of the country of origin.

Every attempt has been made to contact the relevant copyright-holders, but some
were unobtainable. We would be grateful if the appropriate people could contact us.

For Noah and the future Oldfields to come

Looking forward to reading this book together

TABLE OF CONTENTS

ACKNOWLEDGEMENTS

First of all, I'd like to thank John Blake Publishing –
and particularly my editor James Hodgkinson – for
giving me the opportunity to work on these books
and for supporting me throughout. Writing stories for
the next generation of football fans is both an honour
and a pleasure.

I wouldn't be doing this if it wasn't for Tom. I owe
him so much and I'm very grateful for his belief in
me as an author. I feel like Robin setting out on a
solo career after a great partnership with Batman. I
hope I do him (Tom, not Batman) justice with these
new books.

Next up, I want to thank my friends for keeping

me sane during long hours in front of the laptop. Pang, Will, Mills, Doug, John, Charlie – the laughs and the cups of coffee are always appreciated.

I've already thanked my brother but I'm also very grateful to the rest of my family, especially Melissa, Noah and of course Mum and Dad. To my parents, I owe my biggest passions: football and books. They're a real inspiration for everything I do.

Finally, I couldn't have done this without Iona's encouragement and understanding during long, work-filled weekends. Much love to you.

CHAPTER 1

CHAMPION OF ENGLAND

13 May 2012

*Oh Man City, the only football team in all of
Manchester!*
City! City! City!

As he lined up in the tunnel with his teammates,
Sergio could hear the songs of the Manchester City
fans filling the Etihad Stadium. They were always
great supporters but Sergio had never heard them
make this much noise. They had a lot to be excited
about. It was a sunny day and at five o'clock that
afternoon, Manchester City could be the Champions

of England for the first time in forty-four long years. All they had to do was beat QPR at home and they would beat big local rivals Manchester United to first place.

'Remember everyone, this is just a normal match,' Manchester City captain Vincent Kompany told his teammates in the dressing room. He could see that they were nervous and he wanted to keep them calm. 'Stay focused, forget about the Premier League title and let's just win this game!'

Their manager Roberto Mancini usually gave a long team-talk before each game, showing his players the best way to beat their opponents. But on this particular day, Mancini had very little left to say.

'Every single one of you has worked so hard this season – you've been brilliant and you deserve to be Premier League Champions. I want you to enjoy today but I want you to do everything you can to win. I believe in you.'

Sergio tried his best not to think about the pressure, but this was definitely the biggest ninety minutes of his career so far. In his first season in

English football, Sergio already had twenty-two league goals and he was the team's star striker. City needed to score to win the league and Sergio was the man that the fans expected to be the hero.

'How are you feeling, Kun?' Vincent asked, using the nickname that Sergio had been given at the age of two.

'I just want to get out there and play!' he replied, shaking his legs and pumping his fists.

As the game kicked off, Sergio worried that it was going to be a bad day. His first few touches were awful and he couldn't control the ball. Whenever he tried a few tricks, the big QPR defenders tackled him easily.

'Keep going, Kun!' Mancini shouted from the touchline. He needed his superstar to stay positive.

With a few minutes left in the first half, Manchester City finally took the lead. Sergio was one of the first to celebrate with the goalscorer, Pablo Zabaleta, his close friend from Argentina.

'What a time to score!' Sergio shouted. It was only Pablo's third goal in four seasons.

There was a great sense of relief from the home fans around the Etihad Stadium but it didn't last long. In the second half, QPR equalised and then went 2–1 up. It was turning into a nightmare for City – meanwhile Manchester United were beating Sunderland and could be crowned Champions instead. Sergio needed to do something special to save the day as he had done so many times before.

Mancini brought on Edin Džeko and Mario Balotelli to try to find a goal and Sergio feared that he might be taken off. He was having a really bad game and it would be risky to play with three or four strikers. Luckily, however, Mancini kept him on the pitch. Sergio only needed one chance to make a difference and he would fight until the very end.

As Mario came on, Sergio told him his plan: 'They're defending very deep so stay close to me and we'll try the one-two.'

Edin scored a header to make it 2–2 but that wasn't enough in itself to win the league. They needed all three points.

'We can do this!' Vincent screamed and the whole

team believed that, especially Sergio. Even in injury time, he didn't panic. When he got the ball, he looked up and passed it forward to Mario. Mario held the ball up and passed it back to Sergio as he ran quickly into the penalty area. A defender tried to tackle him but he stayed on his feet and hit the ball as hard as he could past the goalkeeper.

Goooooooooaaaaaaaaaaaaaaaaaaaalllllllllllllllllllllllllll ll!!!!

Sergio had scored the winning goal! He took his shirt off and whirled it around his head like a cowboy with a lasso. He raced towards the fans, as his teammates chased him.

'What a goal, Kun – your plan worked!' Mario shouted, jumping on his strike partner. Soon, Sergio was lying at the bottom of a big pile of players. Mancini and the coaches were hugging on the touchline. The crowd were going wild – Manchester City had done it and Sergio had saved the day once again.

Kun Agüero! Kun Agüero! Kun Agüero!

Sergio would never forget those incredible

moments. The game resumed and when the referee blew the final whistle a few seconds later, the real celebrations began. The pitch was soon packed with Manchester City supporters sharing their joy with the players.

Championes, Championes, Olé Olé Olé!

Back in the dressing room, everyone was dancing, singing and spraying beer and champagne. Sergio suddenly felt very tired. What an emotional day – with five minutes to go, Manchester City looked like losing the title after months of hard work. But Sergio had never given up. He had faith in his teammates and he had faith in himself. He was born to play football and win trophies, and Manchester City was the perfect place for him to do that.

When the team went back out on to the pitch for the trophy presentation, the stadium was still completely full. With the red flag of his first club, Independiente, around his shoulders, Sergio collected his medal and then jumped up and down as Vincent lifted the Premier League trophy above his head. Edin was next to hold it and then it was Sergio's turn.

'That trophy's nearly as big as you!' Mario joked.

Later that evening, Sergio sat at the team dinner with his parents, Leo and Adriana. He was so pleased to be able to share his happiness with them. He had come a long way from the dirt pitches of the city of Quilmes and he had so much to thank them for.

'Our son, the hero!' Adriana said with tears in her eyes.

'What a first season in England!' Leo added proudly.

Before he went to sleep, Sergio watched a replay of his goal on the computer. He couldn't really remember the details; it had all been such a blur. The television commentary was his favourite part:

Balotelli...Agüeroooooooooooooooooooooooooooo ooooooooooooooooooooooooooo! I swear you'll never see anything like this ever again.

CHAPTER 2

A BRIGHTER
FUTURE AHEAD

'Sergio, how can you still be hungry?' Adriana asked, shaking her head in disbelief. As she was cleaning the tiny family home, her son crawled across the floor towards her and pulled on her skirt. 'You've already had a bowl of soup and two cups of milk so far today!'

Sergio sat quietly and waited. He was only eighteen months old but he was already eating adult food and lots of it. It cost a lot of money that the young Agüero-Del Castillo family didn't have. Times were hard in Argentina. They couldn't afford to buy cow's milk, and so they bought goat's milk instead.

'Goat's milk makes you fit and healthy,' Leo would

say, lifting his son high into the air. 'You'll be a strong footballer like your dad!' Football was already Sergio's favourite game.

Leo had lost his job at a bakery and so the only way that he could pay for his family was through the sport he loved. Every weekend he played as many football matches as possible to earn money in the local tournaments. He was the best playmaker in the area and everyone wanted him to play for their team.

'Sergio, your dad will be back soon from the football pitch. Hopefully he'll have won lots of money and we can buy you more food,' Adriana said, hanging clothes up to dry. She hated the idea of her son being unhappy but luckily he hardly ever cried. Next, she called to his older sister: 'Jessica, can you go and collect some water please? Be careful – don't fill the container too high because it will be too heavy for you to carry.'

Jessica nodded and walked up the muddy path to their neighbour's house. Adriana sighed; this wasn't the home that she had dreamed of. She and Leo had both grown up in Tucumán in the north of Argentina but when Jessica was born, they travelled to Buenos Aires to find better jobs. They were still only teenagers at the time and their parents had begged them not to leave. Moving to a big, busy city was a real shock but Adriana never gave up.

Leo had built the house they lived in – a single room with bare walls made from cheap bricks and a sheet of metal for a roof. There wasn't any water and there wasn't even a toilet. It was a poor neighbourhood with lots of pollution and crime and they never felt safe. There was a stream running just outside their home and on one occasion, when there was lots of rain, it flooded. Leo, Adriana and Jessica had to move out and live in a school for weeks. They called the area 'The Cave of the Vipers' and it was not a good place to live.

Adriana missed Tucumán and she missed her family. Even so, she tried not to worry about these things. 'Sergio, come and sit here with me,' she said, taking a seat at the plastic picnic table. 'I want to tell you the story of your birth.' The boy put his toys down and crawled towards her. He followed her everywhere but he still couldn't walk.

With Sergio sitting on her lap, she began:

'When I found out I was pregnant, I knew it would be a boy, just as I knew Jessica would be a girl. The first clothes I bought for you were blue. I was young and scared but I loved you. They thought you might arrive very early and so I had to stay in hospital for two months. It was a very long time to be away from Jessica and your dad. There was nothing for me to do except talk to you and tell you that everything would be fine. Eventually, they let me go home and wait for you to arrive.

'It took us nearly three hours to get back to the hospital for your birth. We didn't have enough money to get a taxi and so we took a bus, then a train, then another bus and finally we had to walk up a big hill. I was so tired. Your dad was walking very quickly and I couldn't keep up. At last, we made it and they helped me into a bed. Everything was going well but then the doctor told me, "I'm sorry but your baby is stuck in the wrong position." They wanted to turn you but I thought they might hurt you. In the end, they had to fracture your collarbone, but it's all better now, isn't it?

'You were born and you were healthy and beautiful. I thanked God for looking after us. Your dad was so proud to have a son. As the doctor left, do you know what he said? He said, "This boy will bring you great fortune."'

CHAPTER 3

'KUN' AT 'LA QUINTA'

'Let's go to the *potrero* to watch our dads play!' Cuevita said, taking Sergio's hand and leading him out of the house. Sergio gave a big smile to his friend and started running as fast as his little legs would go.

He was two years old and full of energy. When his new sister, Gabriela, was born, the Agüero-Del Castillo family had moved to Florencio Varela, hoping for better luck in a different part of Buenos Aires. They still lived in a poor neighbourhood with only one bedroom but at least they now had a kitchen and a toilet. Leo had a new job as a taxi driver and they also had friends. Cuevita's

dad, Jorge, played football with Leo in the
local tournaments every Sunday. Jorge was the
experienced goalscorer and Leo was the young
playmaker – they formed a great partnership and
often earned extra money for their families.

The dirt pitch where they played was very close
to Sergio's home. The matches started early in the
morning and went on until late at night. Many
people came to watch and there was always lots of
noise when a team scored a goal or won a penalty.
Sergio could see Leo out on the pitch. 'Papa!' he
shouted out happily but Leo couldn't hear him.
The boy tried waving instead but Leo was too busy
creating goals for Jorge.

Sergio watched his dad for a few more minutes
but then he got bored. Cuevita was playing football
with the older boys by the side of the pitch but
Sergio was too young to join in. Instead, he found
some younger boys rolling around in the dirt. When
the match finished and Leo saw Sergio, he wasn't
very happy.

'You're covered in mud from head to toe – what

have you been doing? Your mum is going to be so angry when she sees you!'

Nevertheless, Leo never stayed mad at Sergio for long. He was a good, happy boy with a brilliant smile and Leo could remember being just like that when he was a child.

It wasn't long before Sergio was playing football out on the *potrero* too.

'Sergio scored some amazing goals today!' Cuevita shouted as they ran back into the house. He had given Sergio a pair of his old boots and he had them tied around his neck with a football tucked under his arm. Cuevita was a really good footballer and he was teaching Sergio lots of great new skills. He could already kick the ball really hard.

'That's great, son!' Leo said without taking his eyes off their new colour TV. Leo and Jorge were watching the Argentina versus Romania game in the 1990 World Cup. Their hero Diego Maradona was back but the team was struggling to qualify for the second round. Sergio sat and watched for a bit but it wasn't as exciting as playing football.

At half-time, Leo and Jorge stopped watching and talked about Sergio.

'I've seen him out there, kicking the ball high up in the air. He's powerful!' said Jorge. 'He puffs his chest out like a frog and swings his leg. One day, he'll be as good as his dad.'

'No, better!' Leo replied with a big grin. He wouldn't put pressure on Sergio but he wanted his son to have the chances that he didn't have. He wanted Sergio to have the chance to be a real football superstar like Diego Maradona.

Half an hour later, Sergio came back into the room and stood there waiting impatiently.

Leo knew what was going on. 'It's nearly over, son, and then you can watch it.'

'Why, what do you want to watch?' Jorge asked Sergio.

'*Kum Kum!*' was the reply but it sounded more like 'Kun Kun' because Sergio couldn't quite say the word yet. It was the only word he did say, though, because it was his favourite thing in the world.

Kum Kum was a Japanese cartoon about a naughty

boy who went on lots of adventures. Sergio never missed the TV show and he even copied the way Kum Kum moved.

'He has the same haircut as Kum Kum!' Leo joked.

'And he behaves like him too!' Adriana added, picking up the toy cars that her son had thrown all over the floor.

Jorge sometimes looked after Sergio when Adriana went to work as a cleaner to earn money for the family. The boy cried every time his mum left but Jorge knew how to calm him down.

'Sergio, shall we watch that cartoon you love?'

'Kun Kun!' Sergio would shout and the tears would stop.

Jorge tried to teach Sergio some new words. They sat together at the table with a book filled with pictures of animals, colours and objects around the house. Jorge pointed at a cow.

'What's that, Sergio?'

'Kun.'

Jorge pointed at a chair.

'What's that, Sergio?'

'Kun.'

Jorge pointed at a yellow sun.

'What's that, Sergio?'

'Kun.'

Jorge laughed. It was no use. 'I give up – I'm going to call you "Kun" from now on!'

CHAPTER 4

LOS EUCALIPTUS

Sergio was very sad to say goodbye to Grandpa Jorge and Cuevita but his family didn't have enough money to live in Florencio Varela anymore. They were moving to Los Eucaliptus, a neighbourhood in the Quilmes district just south of Buenos Aires. On the journey, Sergio was quiet. He didn't want to go somewhere new, where he didn't know anyone and he didn't have anyone to play football with.

'Cheer up, Kun!' Adriana said, pinching his cheek. 'Grandpa will come to see us soon and you'll make lots of new friends, I promise.'

It was only when they arrived at their new home that Sergio became happy again. It was one of many simple houses on Avenida Lamadrid. The bedroom was small and the metal roof was full of holes but the view from their front door was spectacular. Leo laughed when he saw the joy on his son's face.

'That's right, Kun – our new *potrero* is right here!' he said, pointing outside. 'If you take one step out of the door, you're standing at the corner spot!'

The football pitch was the centre of the community. The lines were drawn in chalk but they faded very quickly because people crossed the dirt all day long, carrying shopping and visiting relatives. There were large, old eucalyptus trees along the sides of the pitch and the fruit was always falling. From his front door, Sergio could watch the local footballers running carefully around the fruit so that it didn't hurt their feet. Their close control was amazing.

When a game was over, Sergio went out onto the *potrero* to copy the skills that he had seen. He couldn't wait to put them into action against the other local kids. The family couldn't always afford fresh food for dinner but for Christmas, he was given a new football. It was the best present that he had ever received and he was very careful with it.

'Let's play with your new ball!' one of his new friends said.

Sergio shook his head. 'No way – it'll burst on the *potrero*! Let's use yours instead.'

Unfortunately, Sergio was soon too old to just play all day long; he had to attend nursery school. He hated having to stay inside and listen to the teachers. When Adriana said goodbye every morning, he cried and cried and caused as much trouble as possible.

'Stop that, Kun!' his mum would shout as the boy ran around the room with paint all over his hands. 'I'll be back in the afternoon and then you can play as much football as you like.'

Slowly, Sergio got used to sitting still and by the time he went to primary school, he wasn't as naughty. However, as soon as class ended each day he was the first child out of the building. Either Leo or Adriana would be there waiting for him at the gate.

'Come on!' Sergio said, grabbing their hand and

running home. 'Our football match is starting in a minute!'

Once home, he would throw down his backpack, change out of his school uniform and head straight out to the *potrero*. Every afternoon, Sergio played first to eight goals with his new friends but that could take hours on a small pitch with lots of players. Sometimes they even had to put a time limit on the match if it was getting too dark to see the ball.

It was a big local derby – children from the front rows of houses versus children from the back rows. At first, Sergio played for the front rows and he was often the match-winner. He could dribble past defenders easily and no goalkeeper could save his powerful shot. He may have been small but he was already very strong.

His best friend Cristian played for the other team and for months he tried to get Sergio to switch sides. 'Come and play for us, Kun. With you and me, we would never lose!' he said again and again. Cristian was a very good goalscorer but he needed someone to create more chances for him. Sergio would be perfect. 'Just think about the prize money!'

Like his dad, Sergio was earning money from his football skills, even at the age of five. Each player had to pay a few cents to play and the winning team would earn a peso, enough to buy lots of tasty ice lollies. If he joined Cristian's team, he would always be on the winning team and Sergio loved those ice lollies.

'Okay, I'll play for you!' he finally agreed, and Cristian smiled the biggest smile. They had their brilliant new signing.

Sergio got the ball in the midfield and ran towards the goal, keeping the ball away from the defenders. Cristian made a good run into the penalty area. He opened his mouth to call for the ball but Sergio had already seen him. He played a perfect pass through a crowd of players and Cristian had a simple chance to score.

'Thanks Kun!' he said, giving him a big hug.

Cristian would lose count of the number of times that he said those words to his best friend.

Sometimes he set up goals for Sergio but Sergio was usually the playmaker. He loved the feeling of scoring but he was just as happy when he played an amazing through-ball for one of his teammates. It was a great partnership and they were unbeatable.

CHAPTER 5

FOOTBALL, FOOTBALL, FOOTBALL

Leo took a few deep breaths and a big gulp of water. It was half-time and his team Dardo Rocha were winning 2–0 thanks to their new Number 10. It was the most competitive football that Leo had played in years but he loved it.

'Leo, look at Kun!' said Eduardo, one of his teammates, pointing over to the area behind the goal. Sergio was playing football with the other children. He was the smallest and the youngest but no-one could get the ball off him. The taller boys were getting angry as they chased Sergio around in circles.

Leo laughed. 'He takes after his dad!'

'You're the best player I've ever played with,'

Eduardo told Leo, 'but your son is going to be even better!'

They weren't the only ones who could see that Sergio was a natural talent. Whenever he got the ball, he did something special and made defenders look silly. Sergio could play football all day long – it was what he was born to do. Many youth coaches had asked Leo how old his son was and who he played for.

'It's time for Kun to play at a higher level,' Leo told Adriana one night. 'He needs to challenge himself against better players.'

Jorge Ariza had known about Sergio for years; he had even made the cake for the boy's fourth birthday. In his spare time, 'The Baker' found the best players for Primero de Mayo, a local youth team. One day he went to watch a tournament that his friend Gustavo was playing in. Leo was also playing but it was his son who really caught Jorge's eye.

Sergio was playing beside the pitch with some other children. 'The Baker' watched as he controlled the game, calling out instructions to his teammates and making clever passes to create goals. As soon as the adults' game finished, Jorge ran to Gustavo.

'Who is that kid over there?' he asked, pointing.

'That's Kun Agüero, son of Leo del Castillo,' Gustavo replied. 'He's brilliant, isn't he?'

'He's only six but he already looks like a footballer! He's strong and he understands the game very well.'

Gustavo introduced Jorge to Leo. 'It's really nice to meet you. I was watching your son play football. He just might be even better than you.'

Leo laughed. 'That's what everyone keeps telling me!'

'I'm a scout for Primero de Mayo and I want Kun to come and play for us.'

'How good is your team?' Leo asked. 'Kun is getting a lot of offers. He needs a challenge.'

'It's a very good level of football, I promise,' Jorge replied.

'Okay, I have an idea,' Leo said with a cheeky grin on his face. 'If your team of boys can beat mine, then Kun will sign for you.'

'The Baker' agreed and they set a date for the big

match. Sergio was excited about playing for Primero de Mayo but he also wanted to do his best for his friends. He was competitive and always wanted to win every game. Leo's Los Eucaliptus team did very well but in the end Jorge's Primero de Mayo team were the winners. Afterwards, the two managers shook hands.

'Congratulations,' Leo said, 'Kun is now part of your team!'

Jorge was delighted to look after such a talented young player. He would often pick Sergio up for training. On one occasion, after talking to Leo for a few minutes, Sergio came running into the room, covered in sweat.

'Kun, are you ready to go?' asked 'The Baker'.

'Not yet, the game has gone to penalties!' Sergio replied and then ran back out to the *potrero*. He was earning money by playing against much older boys.

Jorge just laughed. Even after hours of football, Sergio still had the energy to be Primero de Mayo's star player. At practice sessions, Jorge stood with the coaches and listened to their conversations.

'Look at the way he drops deep to get the ball. Where did he learn that?'

'You can see he's thinking one step ahead of everyone else.'

'He was quiet all match and then look what he just did!'

'They try to stop him by fouling but he just gets up and carries on.'

'He's so strong for someone that small – he reminds me of Romário!'

Sergio's best friend Cristian also joined Primero de Mayo and together they helped lift the team from Division C to Division A. Again, Cristian was the top scorer but Sergio was the star player, creating chance after chance for his teammates. For the first time in history, Primero de Mayo won three championships in a row.

Sergio particularly loved free-kicks; he never let anyone else take one. His favourite player was River Plate's Enzo Francescoli, and almost every time the

Uruguayan hit a free-kick, it was a goal. Sergio would practise and practise until he was just as successful as his footballing idol.

Primero de Mayo wasn't the only team that Sergio played for. He was also playing for Loma Alegre and the Independiente youth teams. Everywhere he went, he created goals and won trophies. Word was spreading about his incredible talent. His coaches gave him as much freedom as possible on the pitch. There wasn't much that they could teach him except teamwork and determination.

'Keep going, Kun!' they would shout if Sergio was having a quiet match. All he needed was one chance and he would score. He was always dangerous.

Leo went everywhere with Sergio and never missed a match. He was very proud of his son but he wanted to protect him from injuries.

'Kun, are you sure you want to play so many games?' he asked, even though he knew the answer. Sometimes Sergio played six or seven games in a weekend and he was still only seven years old. 'Don't you feel tired?'

Sergio replied straight away: 'No, Dad, I love football!'

Leo understood his son's passion but something had to change. Sergio played matches all over Buenos Aires and he was too young to travel on his own. So one night at dinner, Leo told his family some big news:

'I've decided to stop playing football.'

Adriana was shocked. 'Are you sure?' she asked. She knew how important the sport was for her husband. He was only twenty-seven and could continue playing for many more years.

Leo nodded. 'I need to focus on the family and on Kun's career.'

The family was growing bigger and bigger. Sergio had a new sister, Daiana, and, for the first time, a brother, Mauricio.

'Kun, I need you to stay in the house because your mum and I will be coming back from the hospital with Mauricio,' Leo told him.

Sergio sat waiting but he quickly got bored and went out to the *potrero* to play. When they returned and found the house was empty, Leo knew exactly where Sergio would be.

'Kun, come here and meet your brother!' he shouted outside.

Sergio ran inside, kissed his mum on the cheek, took one look at Mauricio and said, 'Can I go back out and play now?'

CHAPTER 6

HEROES IN ACTION

Sergio hardly ever watched football; he was too busy *playing* football, which he much preferred. Leo, however, was a big River Plate fan and when they reached the final of the Copa Libertadores, South America's biggest club competition, he was desperate to go. River lost the first leg against Colombia's América de Cali 1–0. The second leg was in Buenos Aires and Sergio was now old enough to join him for the first time.

'Kun, would you like to go and see River Plate play live in a big stadium?' Leo asked, knowing it was a good way to persuade Adriana to let him go. 'It will be an eighth birthday present for you.'

Sergio nodded happily. He couldn't wait to see his heroes Enzo Francescoli and Ariel Ortega in action. Sometimes he listened to matches on the radio or watched them on TV but being there in the crowd would be so much better.

The only problem was that Leo didn't have enough money to buy the expensive tickets and the final was almost sold out. So Leo, Sergio, Cristian and Cristian's dad Daniel set off early in the morning from Quilmes to the Monumental Stadium in Buenos Aires. It was a very cold day and Sergio crossed his fingers in his gloves, hoping that they would still be able to get into the stadium.

'Don't worry, Kun,' Leo said. 'We'll get in, I promise.'

Luckily he was right. As the game kicked off they were still outside but suddenly they heard people selling cheap tickets and Leo raced over to see what he could get. He returned looking disappointed but then his face lit up with a cheeky smile.

'Right, let's go in!' he shouted, holding up enough tickets for all of them.

'Yes!' Sergio was so happy to be going in to see his first ever top-level match. Their timing was perfect; as they got to their seats they had the perfect view of Hernán Crespo scoring for River.

Goooooooooooooooooooooaaaaaaaaaaaaaaaaaalll llllllllllllllll!!!!!!!!!!!!!!!!!!!!!!

The noise was incredible and Sergio was blinded by the big floodlights and the smoke. 'Wow!' was all he could say when they were back in their seats after celebrating the goal. The pitch looked so beautiful from up in the stands, so big and green. Sergio would be dreaming about this for weeks to come.

He watched as Ariel Ortega dribbled past defenders and Francescoli played neat passes across the midfield. On the *potrero*, Sergio and Cristian pretended to be these players every day. Now they were watching the reality and it was even better. Sergio turned to Cristian to say:

'Wouldn't it be amazing to be professional footballers?' he asked, but it wasn't really a question. Cristian nodded without taking his eyes off the game.

There would be plenty of time to talk about it when it was over.

In the second half, Crespo scored again to win the title for River Plate. All of the fans were hugging each other and some were even crying with joy. The singing was the loudest thing Sergio had ever heard. He would never forget that atmosphere.

After the game, the party carried on into the streets of Buenos Aires. Someone passed red–and-white River Plate flags to Sergio and Cristian and they waved them above their heads until their arms got tired. Their throats were sore from all the singing but they refused to stop.

'I'm glad you enjoyed it,' Leo said in the car on the way home. 'I thought you might find it a bit boring to sit still for ninety minutes.'

'How could anyone find that boring, Dad?' Sergio replied, speaking so quickly that Leo could hardly understand him. 'It was amazing! When can we go again? I want to be Crespo when I'm older! I want to score winning goals and hear thousands of fans chanting my name.'

Leo smiled. 'If you keep playing this well, you could be better than Crespo. You could be Maradona!'

CHAPTER 7

CATCHING
THE EYE I

When Sergio and Cristian came in from playing on
the *potrero* one Friday evening, Leo had an invitation
for them.

'Would you two like to go for a trial at Lanús
tomorrow?' he asked. He had already talked to
Cristian's dad, Daniel. Lanús weren't one of the
biggest clubs in Argentina but they were still in the
Primera División.

'Yes please!' Sergio said, jumping up and down
with excitement. If he did well, perhaps one day he
could be like Ortega, Francescoli and Crespo, and
play in front of big crowds. Cristian was thinking the
same thing and had a big smile on his face.

When they arrived at the training pitch, there were at least twenty kids waiting for their chance to impress. The Lanús youth team would be playing against a team of possible new players. Sergio couldn't wait.

'What are your names and positions please?' a man with a clipboard asked them.

'Cristian Formiga, striker.'

'Kun Agüero, Number Ten.'

'Thank you, now please follow the other boys,' the man said, pointing towards the pitch.

It looked at least five times bigger than the *potrero*. They had never played on a full-size pitch before. As they did some warm-up exercises, Sergio looked across at their opponents. The Lanús players looked very professional in their matching kits. They also looked much bigger and stronger.

'They can't be the same age as us!' Sergio said to Cristian.

'No, they're at least eleven years old,' Cristian replied. That was two years older than them. Sergio had never seen him look so nervous.

The man with the clipboard handed everyone a shirt to wear. Cristian had the Number 8, and Sergio had the Number 4 – but he wasn't happy.

'Excuse me, did you give me the wrong shirt?' Sergio asked the man politely.

'No, you'll be starting at right-back,' the coach replied.

'But I'm an attacker – I can't play in defence.'

'Sorry, we have too many attackers. We'll try to swap positions later in the match.'

It was the worst game of Sergio's life. The Lanús left-winger was much taller and Sergio couldn't make a single tackle. He hoped that they would move him forward for the second half but instead he was substituted.

On the journey home, Sergio didn't say a word. Leo had never seen him so angry.

'Sorry Kun, just forget about today,' he said. He was angry too. 'That was a waste of time but they are the ones who have made the mistake.'

A few weeks later, Sergio and Cristian had a successful trial at Quilmes but the families couldn't afford the kit, the travel and the membership fee. Sergio was very disappointed.

'Don't worry, we'll find a team that sees your talent and will pay the money for you,' Leo said with confidence. He knew his son had lots and lots of talent.

A tournament in Luján with Loma Alegre was a great opportunity for Sergio to test himself against the best young players from other cities in Argentina. Loma Alegre beat five teams to reach the final against favourites San Lorenzo. A photo of Sergio was on the front page of the local newspaper and 4,000 fans came to watch the final.

'This is a big day for all of you,' the coach said before the match, looking around at his players. Most of them looked nervous but Sergio was calm. 'If we play as well as we have in the other games, we can win this!'

It was a very close match. With a few minutes to go, it was still 0–0. It was time for some magic. Sergio got the ball on the right and ran down the wing. He looked up and saw that Antonio, the Loma

Alegre striker, was free in the middle. His cross was perfect and Antonio tapped the ball into the goal.

'Thanks Kun!' he shouted as they celebrated the winning goal. At the final whistle, the team did a lap of honour with the trophy. Sergio had another winner's medal for his collection.

For Loma Alegre's next tournament, Cristian was back in the team. Together, Sergio and Cristian were still unstoppable. In the first match, Sergio scored five goals and Cristian scored two. In the final, they scored one goal each in a 2–0 win. As captain, Sergio lifted the trophy high above his head.

Championes, Championes, Olé Olé Olé!

'The other teams looked at you little boys from Quilmes and thought it would be easy,' Leo laughed on the journey home. 'That was a big mistake!'

Everyone was now talking about Sergio as a future star. Leo received lots of offers for his son from top clubs but he had to decide which one was the best. It was only when Cacho Barreiro, the coach of Los Primos, said he wanted to sign Sergio that Leo knew he had found the most suitable option.

'When Kun played against us earlier in the season, he was incredible,' Cacho said when they met for coffee. 'He was the best player I'd ever seen at that age. After the match, we had a meeting – we decided we had to do everything possible to sign him. He's not world class yet but I can help him to get there.'

Leo knew that Cacho was a great coach and always looked after his young players. Sergio was soon a Los Primos player.

'Stay focused, Kun!' Cacho shouted from the sideline. 'The game isn't over yet.'

Los Primos were winning 10–1 but Cacho still wasn't happy. He always wanted more from his players, especially Sergio. Sergio was no longer allowed to play six games each weekend; he had to take care of himself. In one match, he had missed a few good chances and they were 1–0 down. At half-time, Cacho spoke to him:

'Kun, you're showing off too much. It will be your fault if we lose this match.'

With these words in his ears, Sergio scored the

equaliser in the second half. Cacho's plan had worked again.

'That was better,' he said after the final whistle. 'You have so much potential, Kun, but you have to take this seriously. You have to behave like a sportsman. If you listen to me, you'll be Argentina's next great striker.'

CHAPTER 8

EXCITING TIMES AT INDEPENDIENTE

Ricardo Enrique Bochini stood on the touchline at the Independiente de Avellaneda training ground, watching his youngsters play against a tough local team. 'El Bocha' had played for Independiente for many years and he was a real club legend. His job now was to find the best Under-11 players who could move up to the 'El Rojo' youth team. They trained twice a week and then played a match at the weekend. 'El Bocha' had many good players in his squad but only one amazing player.

'Keep going, Kun!' he shouted. Sergio was getting kicked every time he got the ball. Rival teams knew he was their best player and so would try anything to stop him. Sergio just got up and called for the ball again. 'El Bocha' laughed to himself – he had never seen a nine-year-old kid with so much technique and power. The boy's shooting was incredible and his corner kicks reached all the way to the six-yard box. 'El Bocha' watched in wonder as Sergio got the ball, flicked it round his marker and ran towards goal. He already had a hat-trick.

'One day, you will wear my Number Ten shirt at Independiente!' 'El Bocha' told Sergio, and Leo had never seen his son smile so much.

Soon it was time for the selection process. Sergio just hoped he could stand out above the other 200 boys at the trial. Cristian, though, was in no doubt. 'You're the best young player in Argentina, Kun!' he said as they arrived together. Sergio smiled; it was great to have the support of his best friend.

They were organised into teams of eleven – some wearing red bibs and others wearing yellow bibs - and each game lasted ten minutes. Sergio and Cristian would start on the bench for the same team.

'I can't wait to get out there!' Sergio said. He

knew that this was a great opportunity to show the world what he could do. He was ready.

When he came on, they put him as a Number 10. Sergio knew then that it would be a good day. As soon as he got the ball, he ran at the defenders and scored. He didn't stop until the end of the day.

A few days later, Sergio got a phone call asking him to play in a tournament. He was so happy.

'They want me to play for Independiente!' he ran to tell Cristian.

'Me too!' was his reply. They ran around the *potrero* with their shirts over their heads to celebrate.

There were twenty teams at the tournament from all over Argentina. All of the big scouts came to watch to find the next big talents. The coach, Agustín Balbuena, made Sergio the captain and played him in the centre of midfield in his favourite '10' shirt. Leo was there to watch and he was so proud to hear everyone talking about his son.

'Agüero, remember that name,' one scout said to another. 'He's going to be amazing!'

Independiente finished third, with Sergio scoring six goals and creating many more. He attacked well, beating defenders down the left wing with his speed and skill. He had been one of the best players in the tournament and Boca Juniors wanted to sign him. Agustín knew that they had to act fast to keep Sergio at the club.

'Kun was brilliant and we need him in our youth team,' he told Néstor Rambert, the head of the youth teams, as soon as the team returned from the tournament. 'He's a very special talent, I promise.'

Sergio signed for Independiente and it was the happiest day of his life. After years of playing on dirt pitches in Los Eucaliptus, it felt amazing to play on the beautiful green grass pitches at the club's training ground. It was so much easier to control the ball and dribble. Sometimes, the youth team even practised on the pitch next to the first team. That was a dream come true for Sergio.

'Dad, it was amazing!' he said when he got home. 'The professionals were playing so close to us and they looked so big!'

Just when everything was going so well, Sergio got some bad news. They would be moving away from Los Eucaliptus after twelve years, leaving all of their friends and his beloved *potrero* behind. He couldn't believe it.

'The new house is much bigger, Kun,' Adriana told her son but that didn't help. All she wanted was to protect her children from the dangers of alcohol and crime so that they could grow up to have successful and happy lives. 'We'll have two bedrooms, a living room, a kitchen, a bathroom. You'll be able to play football outside the house and Los Eucaliptus is only ten minutes away!'

In the end, it worked out well. He still saw his friends and he was too busy at Independiente to really miss the *potrero*. They were exciting times for Sergio but it was just the beginning.

CHAPTER 9

CATCHING THE EYE II

'Saviola made his debut for River Plate when he was sixteen,' Sergio told Emiliano, his best friend at Independiente, on the way to a match. Javier Saviola was Argentina's new star striker and Sergio wanted to be just like him. He even had the same plain black boots that Saviola wore. 'And he scored – that's what I want to do!'

Emiliano laughed. 'When you score, we'll celebrate together.' For most boys that would have been a crazy dream but for Sergio, it was possible. He was a brilliant, natural talent. He was still playing four matches every Saturday for four different teams but everywhere he went, he scored great goals.

Everyone in Buenos Aires knew the name 'Kun Agüero'.

Sergio's first love, however, was Independiente, where he had formed a great 'little and large' partnership with Emiliano. Emiliano was a very tall goalkeeper and he could kick the ball really far. Whenever he got the ball, he knew exactly where Sergio would be, waiting to dribble past every defender and score.

'Thanks, Emiliano!' Sergio would shout.

If they fouled Sergio in the box, he wouldn't take the penalty. Emiliano would sprint up from his goal and strike the ball powerfully into the net.

'Thanks, Kun!' Emiliano would shout.

They were the two top scorers in the league.

Néstor Rambert was pleased to see his youngsters doing so well but he knew there would be trouble. The newspapers were writing about Sergio's talent, and Boca Juniors and River Plate – the biggest clubs in Argentina – were desperate to sign him. He was only eleven years old but no-one doubted his future.

'I like it here,' Sergio told his dad. 'We have a really good team and Rambert lets me play where I want, between the midfield and attack.'

Néstor would do anything to keep Sergio at Independiente. He even gave Leo a job as kit man so that the family could afford new boots and the bus journeys to training. 'Kun is the future of this club,' Néstor told everyone with total confidence.

At the City of Ayacucho tournament, Independiente reached the final. It was a very close game and they needed their superstar to do something special. Independiente won a free-kick and Sergio went to take it. As he looked at the goal, he thought about his hero Enzo Francescoli. He never missed a chance like this.

Sergio hit the ball powerfully over the wall and past the goalkeeper. He was the hero yet again and his teammates ran to celebrate with him.

Kun! Kun! Kun! Kun!

The more games they played together, the better the team became. To win the league, Independiente would have to beat River Plate in a final match.

It was the most important game of their young lives.

'We can do this!' Sergio told his teammates before kick-off. He was often very quiet but on a day like this, he needed to be a leader.

Miguel Ángel Tojo, the manager of Argentina's national youth teams, was there to watch the big final. He loved to see the country's best young talent playing for fun, still free from the pressures of professional football.

From the kick-off, Independiente took control of the game. Tojo had heard a lot about 'Kun Agüero' but he was still amazed by what he saw. Sergio was small for a twelve-year-old but he had so much strength that much bigger defenders couldn't get the ball off him. Tojo knew all about Sergio's goalscoring but this kid had everything. He could drop deep to get the ball, then dribble down the wing and cross or play a perfect pass through to the striker. By half-time, Independiente were winning 2–0 and Sergio had set up both goals.

'Kun is the best player on the pitch,' Tojo told

Néstor Rambert, who smiled and nodded. 'He's much tougher than he looks and he's very skilful with the ball at his feet.'

The match finished 2–1 and Tojo was so impressed that he did something that he had never done before: he went in to the dressing room to congratulate the players. Sergio was the first player he spoke to.

'What a great performance today!' Tojo said, shaking his hand. 'That was the first time I'd seen you play but I really don't think it will be the last.'

Sergio couldn't stop smiling – not only had they won the league but Argentina's national youth manager had praised him.

Tojo wasn't the only one. The next day, the newspaper wrote about 'a magnificent performance from Independiente's Number 10, Agüero, a player who is sure to have a successful future'. They also talked about Emiliano: 'the team had their goalkeeper to thank for a brilliant display.'

Sergio and Emiliano read the article again and again. They were local celebrities. 'When I score my first goal for the Independiente first team, you'll be our goalkeeper,' Sergio said excitedly, 'and I'll run all the way back to celebrate with you!'

CHAPTER 10

BORN WINNER

When Independiente offered Jorge Rodríguez the chance to coach the Under-14s, he thought about Sergio and said yes. He could remember watching Sergio play three years before, when he dribbled past every defender and scored an amazing goal. Jorge said to his brother, 'This kid is going to be a superstar.'

Jorge was very excited to manage Sergio. The boy would be his star player, in the Number 10 role between midfield and attack, but he needed a few more players to make sure that Independiente won the league again, and so brought in Diego to play in midfield and Pepe to play as a striker. The three boys were soon very good friends.

'Who's your favourite player?' Sergio asked at their first practice. It was a very important question.

'Juan Román Riquelme,' Diego said.

'Javier Saviola,' Pepe said. 'What about you, Kun?'

'I like Riquelme and Saviola, and Francescoli and Ortega. But I think my favourite player is Michael Owen.'

Sergio loved watching the Premier League on TV and Liverpool was his favourite team. Ever since Owen's brilliant goal against Argentina in the 1998 World Cup, he had watched him play whenever he could. Like Sergio, Owen was fast and skilful with a great shot.

'I want to play in the Primera División for Independiente, and then for big clubs in Europe,' Sergio told his new friends. 'And I'll play in lots of World Cups for Argentina!'

His plan was clear but he knew he had to keep working hard. There were lots of good young players in Argentina and he needed to get better and better. Sergio practised his shooting every day and, in his first game of the season, scored a hat-trick.

'Kun, that was amazing!' Diego said at the final whistle. 'Your shot is so powerful that the goalkeeper has no chance. I hardly ever score.'

In the next match, Sergio took the ball past one defender, and then another, and then another. There was just one defender left but he could see Diego in a good position. Instead of going around the last defender, he passed to Diego for an easy goal.

'You scored!' Sergio said, running over to celebrate with his teammate.

'Thanks Kun!' Diego replied.

At first, Jorge tried to give Sergio instructions but he soon realised that it was often best to let Sergio make his own decisions. He was a very intelligent player and he was one step ahead of the others. In one game, it was 1–1 with three minutes to go. Independiente needed to score to win but Sergio was trying to dribble past defenders.

Jorge's brother couldn't believe it. 'You have to tell him to pass the ball back to a teammate!' he shouted, but Jorge shook his head. He knew his superstar would do something special.

Suddenly, Sergio found a tiny bit of space and his fierce shot hit the post and went into the goal. 2–1! When the final whistle went, it was 4–1 and Sergio had scored all four goals. Jorge's brother was speechless.

Miguel Ángel Tojo had been watching a lot of Independiente youth team matches and there were two players that he wanted in his Argentina Under-15 squad. Both would be thrilled.

'I made the team!' Sergio shouted when he heard the news. Leo and Adriana were so proud of their son.

'Me too!' Emiliano shouted. They hugged each other; it would be great to play together for their country.

Before that, though, they still had a league title to win. All Independiente had to do was beat Rosario Central in their last game. It was such an important match that the players stayed overnight in a hotel.

'Wow, this is where the first team stays!' Sergio said, looking at the beautiful hallways and dining rooms. 'I feel like a professional footballer already.'

The team tried to go to bed early but they were too excited to sleep. They couldn't wait to play the final match and win the league. After playing cards for hours, they were finally tired enough to rest.

Sergio was determined to be the hero. As captain, he did feel some pressure to win but he always stayed calm. Early in the game, he got the ball on the left and ran towards goal. He dribbled around one defender and as he broke into the penalty area, another defender fouled him. Penalty!

Emiliano ran up from his goal. He was normally a brilliant penalty-taker but on this day, his shot hit the post. The Independiente players had their heads in their hands but Sergio told them, 'Don't worry, we will have more chances to score!'

With three minutes to go, it was still 1–1. That wasn't enough; Independiente needed a win to take the title. Jorge encouraged his players to go forward and try to score. While his teammates started to panic, Sergio didn't. 'We're going to win but we all need to stay calm,' he tried to tell them – but even so, there wasn't long to go.

Sergio got the ball just past the halfway line. Jorge wanted him to keep it but he passed the ball to Pepe on the right wing. As Pepe dribbled towards the penalty area, Sergio was running towards goal. 'Pepe, I'm here!' he shouted and Pepe crossed it towards him. Sergio stretched out his leg and touched it before the defender. The ball went through the goalkeeper's legs and into the net.

Gooooooooooooooooooooaaaaaaaaaaaaaaaaaaaaaaa aaaaaalllllllllllllllllllllllllllllll!!!!!

Sergio took off his shirt and swung it around his head. What a moment. As his teammates jumped on him, he threw the shirt into the air. When the referee blew the final whistle, the whole team ran from the centre circle and dived onto their bellies.

Everyone was talking about Sergio's match-winning performance but the best part was yet to come. They got to parade the trophy before an Independiente first team match, in front of 27,000 fans. As captain, Sergio led his players out onto the pitch. During their lap of honour, the noise was incredible and there was red smoke everywhere.

SERGIO AGÜERO

Sergio loved Independiente more than ever. He
vowed that one day, he would play on this pitch and
the fans would cheer his name.
Agüero! Agüero! Agüero!
Sergio was sure of that.

72

CHAPTER 11

'NOT BAD FOR A FIFTEEN-YEAR-OLD!'

'Kun, a scout from Juventus spoke to me at your Independiente game yesterday,' Leo said over their family dinner. 'They want to sign you and I said I'd speak to you about it.'

Leo and Adriana had talked for hours about what was best for Sergio. He was still only fourteen years old and a move across the world to Europe would be very difficult. It was an incredible offer – lots of money, plus a big flat and free travel between Italy and Argentina – that could help their son escape from poverty. But the most important thing was what was best for Sergio. They waited to hear what he thought.

'Wow!' Sergio couldn't believe it: a top European club wanted to sign him. It was his dream to one day play in the Champions League. What if he never got this opportunity again?

'Would you come with me?' Sergio asked his parents. He was very young and the idea of leaving his family behind was really scary. He was also really enjoying his time at Independiente. He felt at home and he was developing well in a friendly environment. Moving to Italy could really affect his form on the football pitch. He always played best when he was happy.

'Son, you don't need to decide right now,' Adriana said, giving Sergio a hug. She could see the worry on his face. 'Have a think about it and let us know in a few days.'

In the end, they turned down the Juventus offer. Sergio would grow up in Argentina surrounded by his family and friends. Independiente were delighted.

'Kun, we're so pleased that you've decided to stay,' the club president said with a big smile. 'We look after our best young players and you could be the best of all time!'

It was a relief to have things sorted; now Sergio could focus on his football again, the thing he loved most. But after just one game back in the youth team, things changed again. Guillermo 'Luli' Ríos became the new manager of the Independiente reserves. Luli knew Sergio very well.

'My plan is to bring up some of our youngsters,' Luli told his coaching staff on his first day in the job. 'We have lots of special talent and they need experience.'

Sergio was top of Luli's list and just after his fifteenth birthday, he was called in for a meeting.

'Hi Kun, how's it going?' Luli asked, shaking his hand.

Sergio was trying not to get too excited. 'Good, thanks. Our team hasn't lost a game yet this season!'

'Yes, I've been watching – you're a very impressive team!' the reserves coach said. 'You're the star and we want you to come and train with us.'

Sergio was speechless. He couldn't wait for the

challenge of playing with older, stronger players. He was ready to impress. When he found out that Emiliano had also been asked, the pair of them jumped for joy.

'You're always talking about Saviola scoring on his debut at sixteen,' Emiliano joked. 'You never know, you might make your debut at fifteen!'

Sergio and Emiliano trained with the reserves on the pitch next to the first team. It was a dream come true to be so close to their heroes. They were learning so much.

'That will be us soon,' Sergio said, full of self-belief. Emiliano nodded.

In his first match for the reserves, Sergio came off the bench. He was full of energy and determined to score. With only a few minutes to go, he got his chance. He made a great run behind the defence and suddenly the ball was right in front of him. He ran as fast as he could towards the goal. But just as he was about to shoot, the goalkeeper rushed out and made the save.

Sergio would have nightmares for days. 'I can't

believe I didn't score!' he told his dad over and over again on the journey home.

'I can't either – I've never seen you a miss a chance like that,' Leo replied. 'There's only one way to fix things: score in your next match.'

Sergio came off the bench again but this time, he put the ball in the net. As he celebrated with his new teammates, he pointed towards Leo. He had followed his dad's advice.

A few days later, Sergio was training with the reserves when Oscar Ruggeri, the Independiente first team manager, came over to speak to Luli. Everyone watched and waited.

'I wonder what that's about?' Sergio said.

'Perhaps Ruggeri is looking for new players,' Emiliano suggested.

After a minute, Luli called out, 'Kun, come here!'

Sergio's heart was pounding in his chest. What had he done wrong?

'Kun, this is Oscar Ruggeri,' Luli began but Sergio knew exactly who he was. 'He'd like you to go and train with the first team today – is that okay?'

Again, Sergio was speechless so he just nodded and followed Ruggeri over to the other pitch. He was nervous and excited at the same time. He just hoped he wouldn't make a fool of himself. Sergio was too shy to speak to his heroes but he watched everything they did and tried to copy it.

'How was it?' Emiliano asked him when they were back in the changing room.

'Amazing!' was all Sergio could say.

He was invited to train with the first team again and then at the end of one session, Ruggeri came up to him.

'Well played today, Kun,' he said, and Sergio smiled. 'Would you like to be on the bench against San Lorenzo on Saturday, or are you frightened?'

Everything was happening so fast and Sergio couldn't believe what he was hearing. He tried to make himself sound as confident as possible: 'No, I'm not frightened at all!'

'Dad! Dad!' Sergio shouted as he ran towards the car. 'I've got incredible news!'

'What is it, Kun?' Leo asked. When he heard,

he lifted his son up into the air. 'My son, the Independiente star!'

Back at home, Adriana was worried. 'But you're only fifteen! These big powerful men will kick my boy all game long.'

'I can deal with that!' Sergio replied. He felt like Superman.

Ruggeri told the newspapers that Sergio would definitely come off the bench during the match. There was even more excitement in the family. Leo did some maths.

'You're fifteen years, one month and three days – you'll be the youngest player ever in the history of the Primera División!'

Sergio stayed overnight in a hotel with the squad. To calm his nerves, he played Playstation with his teammates until midnight. Normally he was really good at video games but his hands wouldn't stop shaking.

'Don't worry kid,' defender Gabriel Milito said before they all went to bed. 'You'll be great tomorrow!'

Sergio was too excited to sleep but eventually it was matchday. He felt calm as he travelled to the stadium in the team bus but once he was in the changing room and saw the red '34 Agüero' shirt, the nerves kicked in. This wasn't a dream; he was actually making his Independiente debut.

'Relax!' Gabriel said, putting an arm on his shoulder.

Sergio went through his normal pre-match routine, wrapping a bandage around each of his feet as Leo had taught him. As he ran out onto the pitch, he looked for his parents in the crowd. When Adriana saw him, she burst into tears.

In the second half, Sergio was told to warm up. As he jogged up and down the touchline, he tried to take long, deep breaths. It was just another match, no different to the matches he had played on the *potrero* in Los Eucaliptus. He waited and, finally, Ruggeri told him he would be coming on.

'Play your natural game and don't stop running,' his manager told him, putting his arm round Sergio's shoulders. 'Enjoy it!'

Sergio would never forget the moment that he ran onto the pitch, with the Independiente fans – including Adriana, Leo, Emiliano and 'El Bocha' – cheering him on. He also knew that Cristian, Jorge, Cuevita, 'The Baker' and Cacho would all be watching the game on their TVs and cheering him on.

Sergio did well in his first twenty minutes, causing the defence lots of problems with his speed and skill. Even though Independiente lost 1–0, there would be other games for Sergio to win.

'Well played, Kun,' Ruggeri said as they walked off the pitch. Sergio was fearless and his manager was very impressed. 'Not bad for a fifteen-year-old!'

Sergio handed his first Independiente shirt to Leo and Adriana. 'This is to say thank you for all your support!'

CHAPTER 12

FINDING HIS FEET

'We don't want to rush your progress,' the Independiente coaches kept saying to Sergio. 'You have a really bright future but you're only fifteen years old. You're not ready to play every minute of every game.'

Sergio nodded but he was getting a bit impatient. After his initial taste of first-team football, he wanted more and more. His club were doing badly and he believed that he could help by scoring lots of goals. Coming off the bench for the last twenty minutes didn't give Sergio enough time to save the day.

'Dad, why won't they let me play a full match?'

Sergio asked after another game on the bench. 'When I come on we're often losing and there's nothing I can do.'

'I know, Kun but they're just trying to look after you,' Leo replied. 'Against big, strong defenders a young striker could get a really bad injury. We don't want that, do we?'

Sergio shook his head.

'If you keep working hard and keep learning from the other players, you'll get your chance, I promise.'

Sergio was determined to make the most of his experience in the first team. He always listened to everything his teammates and coaches said and practised hard. There was a lot to learn about being a top professional footballer but he loved being part of the team.

'This is my first time on an airplane!' Sergio admitted to his teammate Fernando as they took their seats. The Independiente squad were travelling to the north of Argentina to get ready for the new season. As they flew through the sky, Sergio looked down at his country below. Everything was so exciting.

When they arrived at the training camp, his teammates decided it was time for an important club ritual. As Sergio sat playing Playstation in his room, they grabbed him and took him outside. They sat him down in a chair and the captain shaved his head.

'Welcome to the team, Kun!' Fernando said, laughing at his smooth head. Sergio didn't mind; with less hair, perhaps he would be even faster.

With so many people giving him great advice, Sergio was getting better and better. Everyone knew he had lots of natural skill but he needed more than that to be a true superstar. Miguel Ángel Tojo, the manager of Argentina's national youth teams, always taught Sergio many useful things about being a striker whenever the boy trained with the Under-17s.

'When you don't have the ball, you can't just stand still,' Tojo told him. 'Movement is very important. You have to be clever. As soon as the midfielder gets the ball, make a run. He might not pass to you but you're creating space for other players.'

Tojo also taught him about different playing styles around the world and different tactics and formations. Sergio always looked forward to his football education. 'What are we studying today, sir?' he joked.

Finally, nearly a year after his debut for Independiente, Sergio was named in the starting eleven against Atlético Rafaela. It was a big day but he was definitely ready.

'I'm an old pro now!' Sergio told his teammates and they all laughed.

Sergio didn't have his best game but step by step he was working towards his aim – to be Independiente's star striker. The club were so pleased with him that they gave him his first professional contract. Sergio was the player that they wanted to build their team around.

'I'm going to get this club to the top of the league,' he said confidently as he signed the paperwork.

For now, however, Sergio was still the future. He

was picked to play for the reserve team against River Plate at the Estadio Monumental.

'This is where I watched my first ever football match,' he told his teammates as they arrived on the bus. 'Crespo scored two goals and River won the Copa Libertadores.'

'That'll be you one day!' Fernando said. Sergio smiled; it was his dream to win the biggest trophies.

As the reserve team warmed up on the pitch, the new coach, Pedro Damián Monzón, looked very nervous. Independiente had sacked lots of managers in the last few years and so he needed to make a good start.

'Don't worry, Pedro,' Sergio said just before kick-off. 'I'll score two goals like Crespo and we'll win.'

Monzón loved Sergio's confidence – it was one of the many things that made him so special. The player was nearly right, too; he scored one and set up the other as Independiente won 2–1.

Monzón hugged Sergio at the final whistle. 'Thanks Kun,' he said. 'What a brilliant performance!'

With three games left in the season, things got

even better for Sergio. Independiente announced a new first-team manager: Pedro Damián Monzón. Monzón was very clear about his plans: 'I want Kun as my striker.'

Sergio started all three games. He loved playing for a manager who really believed in him. Monzón wanted him to dribble with the ball and enjoy himself. In the first match, Sergio got the ball on the left. Instead of passing, he cut inside and ran towards the penalty area. As another defender came towards him, he hit a powerful shot with his right foot. The ball flew into the top corner of the net.

Sergio had scored his first Primera División goal. He ran to the fans to celebrate – it was the most amazing feeling in the world.

'The first of many, Kun!' Fernando shouted as the team jumped on their goalscorer.

When Sergio scored again in the next match, the fans cheered his name. *Agüero! Agüero! Agüero!* He was so proud and so were his parents in the crowd. It had been a brilliant end to the season, but Sergio was already thinking ahead.

SERGIO AGÜERO

'Next season, I want to start every game and score lots of goals,' he told his dad. Leo smiled; nothing could stop his sixteen-year-old son.

CHAPTER 13

LIONEL MESSI

'Welcome back, Kun!' Tojo said as he arrived for another Argentina training camp. The Under-17 South American Championships were coming up in Venezuela and Sergio was really hoping to be in the squad. He knew that Tojo liked him, but he still needed to work hard and impress the coaches.

The Under-20 team had their South American Championships soon too and so they were sharing the camp. Sergio loved learning from older players. One day at dinner, he decided to eat with a group of Under-20 players. Sergio's teammates were too scared to join him and watched from the other side of the room. As he sat down, one of the players was talking about the new football boots that he had bought in the USA.

'I can't wait to show you – they look so amazing!' he said. 'I'll wear them for practice tomorrow.'

The boy had quite long, messy brown hair and although he wasn't very tall, he looked strong. He seemed to be the team leader because his teammates listened carefully to every word he said. He looked very familiar but Sergio couldn't remember his name. Finally, he introduced himself.

'Hi, I'm Kun Agüero. I play for the Under-17s.'

'Hi, we know all about you,' the boy said. 'The Primera División's youngest ever player!'

Sergio smiled. He was pleased that the older players were talking about him.

'I'm Lionel,' the boy said but Sergio needed more information. 'Lionel…?'

'Lionel Messi,' he replied.

Suddenly, Sergio remembered the name. 'Oh, you're the guy at Barcelona! Wow, they say you're going to be their youngest ever first team player.'

Lionel smiled. 'Yes, that's the plan!'

Sergio and Lionel quickly became good friends. Lionel was only a year older than him and they were both famous youngsters who just loved to play football and win. One day, Sergio watched the Under-20 training session. Desperate to learn new skills, Sergio watched with his mouth wide open; Lionel was the best player he had ever seen. A whole team tried to tackle him but they still couldn't get the ball off him.

'It was like the ball was glued to your foot!' he told Lionel afterwards.

'Thanks, it's all about close control and using your body to protect the ball. You should come and play in Europe. That's where all of the best teams and the best coaches are.'

'I know, I'd love to,' Sergio said, thinking about that offer from Juventus. 'But first, I want to do really well here in Argentina.'

The senior team were preparing for the 2006 World Cup in Germany. As part of their training for tournaments, they always played a warm-up match against a team of youth players. When their manager came to ask Tojo to recommend his best players, it didn't take him long to decide.

'My first pick would be Kun Agüero,' Tojo said. 'He's our best player; there's no question about that.'

Sergio was so excited to play against his heroes. A lot of them were at clubs in Europe and so he never played against them in the Argentinian league. Gabriel Milito, his old Independiente teammate, would be defending against him. 'Play without fear,' Sergio said to himself again and again before kick-off. This was a great chance to impress the top players. He just needed to play his natural game and use his skill and speed.

'No Under-17s player has ever scored in one of these matches,' Tojo told him with a smile. He knew exactly how to get the best out of his star player.

'Then I'll be the first!' Sergio replied straightaway with his amazing confidence.

It was a very tough match. Sergio ran and ran but it was very difficult to find space. The senior players were so good at reading the game and intercepting passes. And they were so much stronger that they always won the ball back. 'Be patient,' Sergio said to himself.

Finally, the ball came to him on the left wing. He had enough time to turn and cut inside onto his right foot. As he moved towards the goal, Gabriel ran to tackle him. It was a heavy challenge and it hurt Sergio's leg but he retained the ball. He kept going and as the goalkeeper came out, Sergio knocked it past him into the net.

He had done it, and now every senior player would know exactly who Kun Agüero was. Sergio ran to Tojo to celebrate his goal. Gabriel kicked the grass. He wasn't happy that he had let one of the junior players score against him. It was embarrassing. Tojo saw this and decided to take Sergio off.

'What a goal!' Tojo said, slapping him on the back. 'But that was a big tackle and I think those defenders may be looking for revenge. You're much safer here!'

Lionel had been watching the match from the touchline. 'That goal was awesome, Kun!' he said, giving Sergio a big hug. Sergio was delighted.

CHAPTER 14

WORLD
CUP GLORY

'Try to bend your right knee,' the physio said, moving it very gently.

'No, I can't!' Sergio said, howling with pain. After the glory of scoring against the Argentina senior team, his leg was really hurting. He could hardly stand up. The physio looked worried.

'Kun, I'm afraid it looks like you've torn some cartilage around the knee,' he said. 'It's a serious injury and you'll need an operation and months of rest.'

Sergio couldn't believe it; he would miss the Under-17 South American Championships and maybe even the start of the league season. Leo could see that his son was scared and put an arm around his shoulder.

'Don't worry, we'll get you the best treatment and you'll get better really quickly,' he promised.

After the operation, Sergio worked very hard in the gym to get himself back to fitness. He wanted to be playing for Independiente again as soon as possible.

'Take it easy, Kun!' Leo said. 'Please don't rush back – it might make things a lot worse.'

Sergio was normally very good at listening to advice but he couldn't wait to get back out on the pitch. A lot of people shared his dad's worries but he was soon travelling with the squad again.

'Wake up, Romario!' Sergio's teammate Nicolás Frutos shouted, throwing a pillow at Sergio's head.

Sergio was shocked. 'What? What's going on?' he asked.

'Look, the manager has compared you to Romario!'

Sergio had heard of the great Brazilian striker but he had never seen him play. He preferred Ronaldo. Nicolás showed him a video on the Internet.

'You're both small and strong, and you're both great goalscorers in the penalty area,' he said. 'And you run and dribble like him too!'

It was a nice thing to hear but Sergio was focused on playing football again. After his injury, he was back to coming on as a substitute in the second half. That wouldn't be enough to win him a place with Lionel in the Argentina squad for the Under-20 World Cup. Only twenty-one players would make it, so he needed to do something special, and quickly.

'All I need is one chance and I'll make sure that they never put me back on the bench ever again!' Sergio told Emiliano.

After playing well in practice, he finally got the chance to start. The pressure was on but Sergio loved pressure. He scored two goals and hoped for the best. It was good news; Sergio was selected for the squad.

'We're going to Holland!' he told Lionel excitedly on the phone.

'We're going to win the World Cup!' Lionel replied.

Argentina had a very good team with Ezequiel

Garay and captain Pablo Zabaleta in defence, plus Fernando Gago in midfield and up front, the best young partnership in the world – Lionel Messi and Sergio Agüero. As the juniors in the squad, Lionel and Sergio shared a room and they talked for hours about European football.

At first, Sergio was still a bit nervous around the older players but Pablo made sure that everyone was relaxed by playing lots of practical jokes. There were lots of Playstation competitions too, especially between Sergio and Lionel. Sometimes they made so much noise that the coaches had to come and stop them. Tojo, however, was very pleased to see his young strikers getting on so well.

'If they're friends off the pitch, they'll be friends on the pitch,' he said happily.

Just before the tournament started, Sergio received some very bad news about another of his best friends. Emiliano had been injured in a terrible car accident. He was in hospital and everyone was very worried.

'What should I do?' Sergio asked Tojo once he had

calmed down a little. For once, he couldn't focus on football. 'Should I go back to Argentina to visit him?'

Tojo put an arm around his player's shoulder. 'For now, we just have to hope that he gets better. I know Emiliano wouldn't want you to miss this tournament.'

Sergio only came off the bench twice in Argentina's first five matches. He understood that he was younger than his teammates and he was enjoying learning a lot from the tournament experience, but he was desperate to make his mark and help his country.

'The semi-final is so important and then if we get to the final, that's even more important,' he told Messi with a sad look on his face after the quarter-final win over Spain. 'There's no way that the coach will let me play in those games.'

'Just wait and see,' Lionel said. 'You never know what will happen.'

The next day, Lionel was surfing the Internet when he saw that Emiliano had died. When Sergio heard the news, he just sat in silence. He couldn't

believe that his friend and teammate was gone.
He thought about all of the great times that they'd
shared at Independiente, all of the penalties that he'd
won for Emiliano to score. What a partnership they
had been.

'No, no, no,' Sergio said eventually with tears
streaming down his face. He was so far from home
and so far from Emiliano. Lionel hugged him and
they cried together.

'Kun, would you like to go back to Argentina?'
Tojo asked. 'You should be with your family at a
difficult time like this.'

Sergio thought for a minute. 'No, you're right –
Emiliano would want me to stay and beat Brazil.'

He came on for the last ten minutes in the semi-
final. It was 1–1 thanks to Lionel's goal but Argentina
needed a winner. Leo dribbled past two defenders
on the left wing and looked for Sergio in the middle.
The ball came across the goal but Sergio couldn't
quite kick it properly. Luckily, Pablo was there to
score.

'We're in the final!' they all sang, dancing around

the pitch as one big group. Together they would win the World Cup for Emiliano.

In the final against Nigeria, the score was 1–1 early in the second half. Suddenly, Sergio got the call.

'Kun, you're going on!'

Sergio was so excited; he would have plenty of time to try to score the winner. As he ran on, he took a couple of deep breaths and focused on the match. Lionel was playing brilliantly, so Sergio needed to get in good positions for his friend to pass to him.

Soon, Lionel gave him the ball and Sergio ran towards goal. He knocked the ball past the defender and kept going. The defender couldn't keep up and so he fouled Sergio. Penalty!

'Great work!' Lionel said as he helped Sergio to his feet and picked up the ball. Lionel took the spot-kick perfectly – they were winning. At the final whistle, they hugged and jumped around the pitch. Sergio cried and cried for his great, much-missed friend. Under his football shirt he wore a T-shirt with the words on it: 'For You Emiliano'.

'World Cup champions!' Sergio shouted. He liked

the sound of those words and he loved the feel of the trophy in his hands.

Lionel was the player of the tournament but Sergio had learnt a lot from his time in Holland. He had also made some great friends, who he would soon play with in the senior team.

CHAPTER 15

'FOR YOU, EMILIANO'

As he sat in the dressing room before kick-off, Sergio reached into his kitbag and took out a white T-shirt. Normally, he didn't wear anything under his red Independiente shirt but today was special. It was Avellaneda's local derby against rival club Racing and he had a very important job to do: score a goal.

He had scored a lot of goals since Independiente gave him the famous Number 10 shirt at the start of the season.

'El Bocha', Sergio's old coach for the Under-11s, handed him the shirt. 'Didn't I tell you that you'd wear this one day?' he said. Now seventeen, Sergio

was seen as the future of the club. He was so proud
to follow in such amazing footsteps.

The shirt had brought him luck so far but today he
needed it more than ever. Sergio had a big promise
to keep.

'Are you ready for this?' his strike partner Nicolás
asked him in the tunnel. They could barely hear each
other because the fans were cheering so loudly.

'Always,' Sergio replied, looking as calm as ever.

With less than ten minutes to go, Nicolás had a
hat-trick and Independiente were winning 3–0. But
Sergio still didn't have his goal.

'It's time to make that dream come true,' he said
to himself as the match kicked off again. He was so
determined to score.

The goalkeeper kicked the ball to Sergio and he
controlled it perfectly. A defender approached him
but with a burst of speed, Sergio ran straight past
him. There was so much space ahead of him. Sergio
ran towards goal with the noise of the crowd in his
ears and with memories of Emiliano in his head
and heart.

A defender stood waiting for him on the edge of the penalty area. Sergio used his skill to take the ball around him on the left and then cut back inside. As the defender dived in for the tackle, Sergio moved the ball to the left again with some magical footwork. The dizzy defender tried to block his shot but it was too powerful. It rocketed past the goalkeeper and into the net.

Goooooooooooooooooooooooooaaaaaaaaaaaaaaaa aaaalll!!!!!!

Agüero! Agüero! Agüero!

Sergio had done it with one of the best goals that the Independiente fans had ever seen. His heart was beating so fast in his chest. He ripped off his red shirt to show the same white T-shirt that he had worn in the Under-20 World Cup Final – 'For You Emiliano' it said. Years ago, he had promised Emiliano that when he scored in the derby against Racing, they would celebrate together. Now he swung his Independiente shirt above his head and then kissed it. His teammates lifted him high into the air and he pointed and cheered towards the sky.

It was another football moment that Sergio would never forget.

The next day, his face was on the back page of every Argentinian newspaper. As he looked through them with his family, Sergio still couldn't believe that he had scored such a beautiful goal.

'Which is your favourite, Kun?' Mauricio asked. He loved being able to boast about his older brother at school.

Sergio shrugged. 'I love them all!'

The praise didn't stop there. Sergio and Lionel Messi were the joint winners of Argentina's 'Golden Newcomer' award. With the two of them in attack, the future looked bright for the national team.

'You better get used to this attention,' his dad warned with a smile.

Every defender in the Primera División now knew the name 'Agüero' and they tried everything to stop him. He was quicker and more skilful than them, so they had to use their strength and experience instead. Every game, Sergio got kicked and pushed and mocked for being young and small. He tried to ignore it but sometimes he complained to the referee.

'What a crybaby!' defenders would shout. 'Why don't you get your mummy to help you!'

Usually, Sergio's answer was to score goals but against Tiro Federal he couldn't find the net. And every time he got the ball, his marker insulted him and shoved him.

'Just let it go,' Nicolás told Sergio. He could see that his strike partner was getting very frustrated. 'He's trying to get you sent off.'

Sergio was usually very quiet on the pitch but this time he'd had enough. He insulted his marker back and the referee told them both to calm down. The Independiente manager decided that it was time to take his star player off but as Sergio walked towards the touchline, his marker was still insulting him:

'Are you too scared to play with the big boys? You're weak.'

Sergio turned around and pushed him. He couldn't stop himself. The defender threw himself to the ground and the referee showed Sergio a red card. He kicked at the grass as he left the pitch. He had made a big mistake.

After the match, he apologised to his teammates. 'I'm sorry, that was really stupid,' he said. 'I let you down today but I promise that won't happen again.'

'Don't worry,' Nicolás said, patting him on the back. 'You're still young and you're learning.'

'Next time that happens, let me know and I'll sort it out!' Lucas joked. He was a tough character who always looked after his young teammates.

Sergio laughed. It was a good reminder that he wasn't the complete player yet. True superstars had to deal with lots of pressure and stay focused at all times.

CHAPTER 16

SIGNING FOR ATLÉTICO

Toni Muñoz sat in his office reading reports from his youth scouts around the world. The sporting director of Atlético Madrid was always looking for the next big thing. The top teams in Europe were trying to buy Atlético's superstar Fernando Torres and so signing a new striker was the club's number-one aim. Since the Under-20 World Cup in Holland, Toni had been hearing lots about a very young Argentinian.

'Kun Agüero could be as good as Lionel Messi,' his South American scouts told him excitedly. 'He's a very clever attacker and he scores goals for fun. We need to sign him before someone else does!'

'I really like what I see in the videos,' Toni replied, 'but I want to see Agüero in person.'

On his first trip to Argentina, Toni watched Sergio play in two matches. He scored one goal and caused lots of problems for defenders. Toni was impressed but he wasn't totally sure. Lots of other clubs were interested in Sergio and if Atlético were going to pay lots of money, Toni needed to be certain.

'Independiente aren't playing well and he has been injured for the last few weeks,' the scouts told him. They knew it would be a big mistake if Atlético didn't sign Sergio. 'You should come back and watch him when he's fully fit!'

Toni returned to Argentina seven months later and this time he was amazed by what he saw. Sergio looked like a world-class striker. He was brilliant at shooting but he also had the skill to create goals out of nothing. Every time he got the ball, the Independiente fans became excited and the opposition defenders got nervous.

'He looks a lot stronger now,' Toni told his scouts. Watching a young player getting better and better was his favourite feeling in the world. It wasn't about the money or the glory; it was about the passion, the beauty and the joy. 'Players can't push him around anymore – he's the real deal now!'

He was right; Sergio had taken another big step towards greatness. He would never be the tallest footballer but he was determined to be the best. Thanks to his match-winning goals, he was now one of the most famous players in Argentina. Everywhere he went, fans stopped and asked him for autographs. Sergio loved the attention as he drove around Buenos Aires in his brand new black Chevrolet car.

'They're calling it "Agüeromania"!' his brother Mauricio told him. Sergio laughed. He was really just a normal seventeen-year-old boy who liked to play video games and go to the cinema with his friends.

When he got back to Spain, Toni wrote a very positive report: 'Kun Agüero is still very young and he would be an expensive signing but I believe he has the potential to be one of the best strikers in the world.'

More and more scouts from top European clubs

came to watch Sergio play and he loved to entertain. In the derby match against Racing, he had taken the ball and dribbled past both central defenders before shooting past the goalkeeper. It was a great goal but Sergio wasn't finished. Three minutes later, he was on the run again. As the goalkeeper came to close him down, Sergio pretended to shoot. As he dived to the floor, Sergio calmly kicked the ball into the other corner of the net.

'You're playing with so much confidence now!' Nicolás told his strike partner as they celebrated his second goal. He had always known that Sergio was destined for bigger and better things.

Toni was watching the match on TV back in Madrid. He wasn't surprised but he was very excited. 'We need to sign Agüero quickly!' he told himself before making some important phone calls.

Independiente really didn't want to sell their star player but they were in a lot of debt. If they could get a big transfer fee for Sergio, it would really help the club. Sergio was very excited about the idea of playing in Europe. He couldn't wait to play against amazing teams like Barcelona, who Leo played for.

'I love playing football here in Argentina but I think I'm ready for a new challenge,' he told his dad.

'I understand, Kun, and there are a lot of clubs that want you,' Leo said before listing the best ones. 'Juventus, Inter Milan, Manchester United, Chelsea, Real Madrid, Atlético Madrid…'

'Wow!' Sergio couldn't believe it. They were the biggest clubs in Europe, in the world. Sergio loved watching them in the Champions League on TV and now he might get the chance to join them. While other clubs were still deciding, Atlético Madrid made their first bid for Sergio. Independiente said no but Toni wouldn't give up.

'We've got to keep going until they say yes!' he told the club's chief executive, Miguel Ángel Gil Marín.

Eventually, Independiente and Atlético Madrid agreed a price of £20 million. It was the biggest fee in the history of Argentinian club football and the most money that Atlético had ever paid for a player.

'He's worth it, I promise!' Toni told everyone with total confidence.

Sergio wasn't worried about the pressure either. 'Spanish football is quite similar to Argentinian football and there won't be any language problems for me,' he told his mum. 'Plus Atlético have other Argentinian players so I'll feel right at home.'

'But if you don't like it, you can just come home!' Adriana said. She was very worried about her young son going to Europe without his family. He wasn't even eighteen years old yet and he had never been to Spain.

'This is the best thing for you,' Leo told him. He would miss his son very much but this was a big step for his career. 'You will learn so much by playing with such great players.'

The Independiente fans were very sad to see their hero leave. In Sergio's last game at the Estadio Libertadores de América, they stood and waved flags that said 'Thank you Kun'. They chanted his name again and again.

Agüero! Agüero! Agüero!

Sergio clapped and waved to the supporters, and then he took off his shirt and threw it into the crowd. He would really miss his first and favourite football club and he would return one day – but it was time for a big new adventure in Europe.

CHAPTER 17

EARLY DAYS IN SPAIN

'Agüero is one of the most important signings in the history of Atlético Madrid,' Miguel Ángel Gil Marín told the Spanish media. 'The fans are going to love him!'

Sergio was standing next to him in a smart black jacket with a big gold necklace around his neck. He looked like the young superstar that he was. 'I hope to have lots of success here,' he said with a big smile on his face, 'and score lots of goals.' He was more nervous than he ever was on the football pitch.

Finally, it was time for the main event. Sergio had swapped the red shirt of Independiente for the red-and-white stripes of Atlético Madrid. He held his new shirt up to the cameras with 'AGÜERO' written in big blue letters. Then he put the shirt on and went out on to the pitch for more photos. There were thousands of fans in the stadium waiting to welcome him, just as there had been at the airport.

Leo and Adriana had travelled to Madrid with Sergio to help him settle in. When they stepped off the plane, the airport was full of Atlético fans desperate to meet their new striker. They already had songs for him and shirts with his name on the back. Sergio couldn't believe it.

'They're crazy!' he said to his parents. 'I think I'm going to love it here!'

When Leo and Adriana went back home to Buenos Aires, Sergio's teammate and fellow Argentinian Maxi Rodríguez was there to look after their son. He invited Sergio to his house for barbecues and they listened to Argentinian music and drank *Mate* tea together.

'I've been here for nearly seven years now,' Maxi told him as he cooked the steaks. 'It can take a little while to adapt to a new country, especially when you're so young. If there's anything I can help you with, just ask. We're neighbours so just shout over the fence!'

It was nice for Sergio to talk to someone who had been through the same experience. It made everything a little less scary. Maxi was from Rosario, like Lionel, and they knew lots of the same players. Maxi had also played at the 2006 World Cup for Argentina and scored the best goal of the whole tournament.

'The fans will expect me to score goals like that every week now!' he joked.

When the season started, Sergio was given his favourite Number 10 shirt, next to Atlético's beloved Number 9.

'They want me to partner Fernando Torres!' Sergio told his parents on the phone. He had been watching Fernando on TV for the last few years and he was one of Sergio's favourite players. He couldn't wait to play with him. 'Together, we're going to score so many goals!'

But Sergio didn't get the brilliant start that he was

hoping for. In the first month of the 2006–07 season, he was only used as a substitute. The fans and the media wanted to see more of Atlético's expensive new striker.

'We don't want to rush you, Kun,' the manager kept telling him but Sergio was desperate to play the full ninety minutes. He needed more time to score his first goal for the club and show that he was ready to play every game.

Finally, Sergio was named in the starting line-up when Fernando couldn't play. 'This is your opportunity – don't waste it,' Fernando told him before the game against Athletic Bilbao. His teammate was always helping Sergio and giving him advice.

As he lined up on the pitch before kick-off, Sergio didn't feel any pressure. He knew that it was going to be a great day. Every time he got the ball, he attacked the goal. In the second half, Atlético had the ball and Sergio was running into space behind the defence. He was far too quick for them. As he got the ball, he could see that a defender was coming across to tackle him, so he cleverly flicked it away from him. Another defender was coming. Sergio was still outside the penalty area but he had no choice but to shoot. He hit the ball so powerfully that the goalkeeper couldn't stop it from going in the net.

Goooooooooooooooooooooooaaaaaaaaaaaaaaaa aaaaaaaaaaaaaallllllllllllllllllll!!!!!

Sergio was so relieved to score his first goal for the club. He ran towards the fans, who were waving handkerchiefs to show love for their new hero. All of his teammates joined him.

'There's no stopping you now!' Maxi said as they celebrated together.

The only thing stopping him was the fouling. Because he was a small young striker, big defenders loved to kick him when the referee wasn't looking. The Atlético coaches were worried that Sergio would get injured but he was used to rough treatment.

'Don't worry,' Sergio joked, 'I played in the Argentinian league at the age of fifteen – I know all about fouls!'

Sometimes Sergio played like he was still in

Argentina. The Spanish fans loved him to play with his natural style but they got angry if he showed off too much when there was a better, simpler option.

'You'll learn about these things,' Fernando told Sergio. 'It's all about picking the right moments to do your skills. As long as you get goals, the fans will forgive you!'

In his first season in Spanish football, Sergio scored seven goals. Some of them had been spectacular but he wasn't satisfied. 'I'm not new anymore. Atlético paid a lot of money for me and it's time to start scoring like I did for Independiente.'

First, however, he had another Under-20 World Cup to play for Argentina, this time in Canada.

CHAPTER 18

THE AGÜERO SHOW

'Wow, you've grown up!' Hugo Tocalli, the Under-20 coach, said when Sergio arrived at their training camp in Argentina. 'The last time I saw you, you were a boy and now you're a man!'

Sergio laughed. After a season in Europe, he did feel like a more mature and experienced player. Plus, he was now a full Argentinian international. When he was called up to the senior squad for a friendly match against Brazil, Sergio jumped for joy. It was a dream come true.

'I'll be playing with all my heroes – Javier Saviola, Carlos Tevez, Juan Román Riquelme!' he told his dad happily on the phone.

Sergio loved training with Javier and Carlos because they gave him lots of advice on how to improve as a striker. He still had a lot to learn about finding space in difficult matches and always being in the right place at the right time.

'You have to be like a hunter,' Javier joked. 'When you can smell a goal coming, get there as fast as you can!'

Sergio played the last half hour of the match and he loved every minute of it. Running onto the pitch in the famous blue-and-white striped shirt was the best feeling in the world.

'Enjoy yourself!' Carlos shouted as he came off the field. Sergio did enjoy himself, even though Argentina lost 3–0. He hoped to play lots more matches for the senior team but for now, Sergio wanted a second Under-20 World Cup winner's medal.

Tocalli was very impressed by Sergio and he could see that he was popular in the squad. There were other very good players including Ángel Di María but Sergio was the one that all of the other players listened to.

With Lionel Messi playing at the Copa América for the senior team, Tocalli decided that Sergio would be his star player. At the end of the last practice before the tournament, he held up the Number 10 shirt. 'This is for you. Kun, last time in Holland you were the baby of the team but this time, you're the leader.'

Sergio was delighted and he couldn't wait for the matches to begin. 'Don't worry, I won't let you down!' he said.

After a tiring flight to Canada, the team settled in Ottawa for the group stage games. Sergio liked exploring new places and meeting people from lots of different countries. Travel was one of the great things about being a professional footballer. There was an exciting atmosphere around the city as fans prepared to watch the world's next big talents. Sergio was right at the top of that list but this was a great opportunity to confirm his reputation.

After a goalless draw, Argentina won their second match 6–0 and Sergio scored two goals. But in the next game, the team didn't play well at all. Sergio won the game with a brilliant free-kick but Tocalli wasn't happy with his players.

'I'm sorry, Coach,' Sergio said. 'We're going to have a meeting and work out what went wrong.'

Tocalli trusted his leader to sort things out and in the next match against Poland, the team were much better. Sergio got two more goals. For the first, he flicked the ball over the defender's head and volleyed it into the net with his left foot. It was one of his favourite goals of all time. Sergio was determined to be the top scorer in the tournament, and the best player too.

'Well done, Kun!' Tocalli said at the final whistle, giving Sergio a big hug. 'I don't know what you said to the other players but it worked!'

'They're calling it "The Agüero Show"!' Leo told him on the phone. He was so proud of how well his son was playing. 'Just three more wins to go!'

Sergio didn't score in the quarter-final or the semi-final but he helped his team to win both matches. In the final, Argentina played the Czech Republic.

'They beat Spain so they must be really good,'

Sergio told his teammates. He was the captain for the final. It would be a difficult match and they would have to play very well. 'But we can win this!'

In the 2005 final, Lionel had been the star. Now it was Sergio's turn to shine. Argentina were losing 1–0 but he never gave up. Éver Banega had the ball in midfield and Sergio saw that there was lots of space between the Czech central defenders. He pointed to where he wanted the ball and the pass was perfect. When he was younger, Sergio might have hit a really powerful shot but this time, he calmly placed the ball into the corner of the net.

'Come on, let's win this!' he shouted as they ran back for the restart. With five minutes to go, Argentina scored a winner. The celebrations were amazing.

Sergio had his second winner's medal. He also won the Golden Boot for top goalscorer and the Golden Ball for best player.

'Anything Lionel can do, I can do too!' he joked as he walked around the pitch holding all three awards.

Once the party was over, Sergio started to think

about the season ahead at Atlético Madrid. 'My aim is twenty goals,' he told Leo confidently.

'Are you sure, Kun?' his dad asked. He didn't want his son to put too much pressure on himself. 'That's a lot of goals!'

'I know but I can do it!'

There was no stopping Sergio now.

CHAPTER 19

DEADLY DUO

The ball came to Sergio on the edge of the penalty area with his back to goal. His first touch was good and he turned quickly and shot with his left foot. The Lokomotiv Moscow defenders stood and watched as the ball flew past the goalkeeper. Sergio was enjoying the UEFA Cup.

'What a goal!' Diego Forlán shouted. Fernando Torres had been sold to Liverpool but Atlético Madrid's new strikeforce looked just as good. Early in the second half, a defender played the ball up to Sergio. He could see Diego making a great run towards goal and so he flicked it on perfectly with his head.

'Thanks, Kun!' Diego said, giving Sergio a big hug as they celebrated another goal.

But with five minutes left, Atlético were losing 3–2. Sergio didn't panic; he just needed one more chance. In the penalty area he was too quick for the Lokomotiv defenders and he lifted the ball over the goalkeeper and into the net. Sergio ran towards the Atlético fans with his arms in the air. They had a new hero.

Agüero! Agüero! Agüero!

Everything was going really well for Sergio. He was playing regularly for the Argentina senior team and he won the 'Golden Boy' prize for the best young footballer playing in Europe.

'Anything Lionel can do, I can do too!' Sergio thought yet again as he lifted the big trophy. At the same posh event in Switzerland, Lionel came second in the FIFA World Player of the Year award. That was Sergio's next aim.

In the Spanish League, Atlético were in fourth position. If they could stay there, they would qualify for the Champions League.

'We can do this!' Sergio told his teammates before their big game against Barcelona. When he first arrived in Madrid, he had been very quiet and shy but now he was becoming one of the team leaders.

Ronaldinho scored a brilliant overhead kick but Sergio was so determined to win. His shot deflected off Carles Puyol to make it 1–1. He set up a goal for Maxi with a brilliant pass and then he won a penalty when Puyol fouled him. Diego scored the penalty but Sergio wasn't finished. He showed his strength to win the ball and then used his skill to dribble past Puyol. From just inside the penalty area, Sergio hit the ball into the bottom corner.

Goooooooooooooooaaaaaaaaaaaaaaaaaaaaaalllllllll llllllllllllllllllllllll!!!!!!!!!!!!!!!!!!!

Sergio was so happy that he took off his shirt and threw it towards the fans.

'What a performance!' Lionel said as they met after the game. He had been on the bench because of an injury. 'I've never seen anyone play like that against Barca – Carles will have nightmares for weeks!'

Sergio loved scoring important goals in important matches. He was getting better and better.

'Dad, do you remember the target I set myself at the start of the season?' Sergio asked at the end of the season. Thanks to him, Atlético would play in the Champions League next year.

'Of course – you said you wanted twenty goals,' Leo replied. 'And how many did you score?'

Sergio had a big smile on his face. 'Twenty-seven!'

He was soon thinking ahead to his next aim – a gold medal at the 2008 Olympics in Beijing. They had a brilliant team with Pablo Zabaleta in defence, Juan Román Riquelme and Ángel Di María in midfield, plus the best young strikeforce in the world: Sergio and Lionel.

'We're going to score so many goals together!' Lionel said.

Unfortunately, Sergio didn't start the tournament very well. After a long club season, he was tired and he just couldn't find the net. Lionel was scoring and the team was winning but Sergio was worried that he might be dropped.

'Don't worry!' Lionel told him. 'You'll find your top form soon – we all know how brilliant you are.'

Sergio never gave up. In the semi-finals, Argentina played their great rivals Brazil. He was desperate to do well, especially with the legendary Diego Maradona, soon to be manager, watching in the stands. In the second half, Ángel played a perfect cross into the box. It was too high for Sergio to use his feet and too low for him to use his head. So he used his body to get the ball into the net.

'I call that the "Chest of God"!' he joked to Lionel as they celebrated the goal.

With his confidence back, Sergio scored again and won a penalty to make it 3–0. In the final, Argentina beat Nigeria 1–0.

'Another medal!' Sergio said to Lionel as they danced around the pitch after the game. When they played together, they always seemed to win.

For his club, Sergio's partnership with Diego was very successful too. They particularly enjoyed playing against Lionel's Barcelona. At home at the Vicente Calderón Stadium, Atlético were 2–0 down.

When Diego scored a brilliant goal, he shouted, 'Let's win this!'

A few minutes later, Sergio ran past the Barcelona defenders; they just couldn't keep up with him. He was slightly off balance and it was a difficult angle for the shot but he scored with a perfect finish. Barcelona scored but Diego equalised from the penalty spot. They needed a winning goal and Sergio was the perfect man for the job.

With four minutes left, Sergio played a one-two and ran into the penalty area. He took the ball past Puyol yet again and shot past the goalkeeper. Sergio ran along the touchline pumping his fists as the fans went wild. He loved being the hero.

'A game is never over when you have Kun in your team!' Diego said at the final whistle as they clapped their amazing supporters.

'He only starts playing properly in the last ten minutes!' Maxi joked but he didn't know what the team would do if Sergio ever left. He was such an important player for the club.

In 2010, Atlético reached the final of the Europa

League in Hamburg, Germany. Sergio had scored six goals in the competition already and he was desperate to win a big club trophy.

'So far, I've only won the Intertoto Cup,' he said to Diego as they waited in the tunnel. He wasn't nervous; he just wanted to play and score. Sergio loved big matches like this. 'Fulham are in really good form but this is a great chance for us.'

After half an hour, Sergio received the ball on the edge of the penalty area with his back to goal. He chested the ball down and turned to shoot. Normally this was one of his best skills but this time, his left foot strike was heading a long way wide of the goal. Luckily, Diego was there to direct the ball into the net.

'Thanks, Kun!' Diego shouted. Sergio was too embarrassed to admit that it had been a shot rather than a pass.

Fulham equalised and the match went to extra-time. Sergio was exhausted but he knew that his teammates were relying on him to do something special. The big, shining trophy was sitting in front of the tunnel; he had been dreaming about it for weeks.

Sergio had lots of chances to score but he just couldn't find the net. He would have to create a goal for Diego instead. With five minutes to go, Sergio dribbled at the Fulham right-back from near the corner flag. Diego was the only Atlético player in the penalty area but Sergio knew exactly how to find him. He hit a perfect ball across the six-yard box and his strike partner tapped it into the net.

Gooooooooooooooooooooooooooaaaaaaaaaaaaaaa aaaaaallllllllllllllllllllllllllllll!!!!!

Diego and Sergio celebrated by diving across the grass. In the stands, the Atlético fans chanted their names louder than ever. It was such a popular partnership. After the final whistle, and wrapped in an Argentinian flag, Sergio danced around the pitch with his teammates. It was a very happy night for the club, the players and the supporters.

Forza Atleti Ale! Forza Atleti Ale! Forza Atleti Ale!

Lifting the Europa League trophy was one of the best moments of Sergio's career but he was hungry for more. He wanted to challenge for the Champions League, even if that meant leaving Atlético. After each match-winning performance, people talked more and more about Sergio but the club really didn't want to sell him. They put a £50 million price tag on their star player.

CHAPTER 20

WORLD CUP HEARTBREAK

After two Under-20 World Cup wins and an Olympic Gold, Argentina were one of the favourites to win the 2010 World Cup. Would defences be able to stop Lionel and Sergio?

'It's time to win another trophy together!' Lionel said as he travelled to South Africa with Sergio, Pablo and Ángel.

'I just hope I get to play!' Sergio replied. He was one of the top strikers in Europe but Argentina had lots of great strikers. Lionel would play every game but Sergio was competing with Manchester City's Carlos Tevez, Inter Milan's Diego Milito and Real Madrid's Gonzalo Higuaín to be his partner. At only twenty-two years old, Sergio was the youngest. It would be very difficult but he always believed in himself.

The atmosphere at the World Cup was amazing. The Olympics had been a great experience but this was so much better. Everywhere he went, Sergio saw the bright colours and flags of thirty-two different nations, and heard the sounds of drums, singing and vuvuzelas. It was one big international party.

Unfortunately, Sergio didn't play in Argentina's first match. He watched from the bench as they beat Nigeria 1–0.

'You'll play the next game, Kun,' Leo reassured him on the phone. 'Carlos, Gonzalo and Diego all got their chance and none of them could score! It's your turn next.'

Sergio hoped his dad was right. Carlos Tevez and Gonzalo Higuaín started against South Korea but with barely twenty minutes to go, Sergio came on to replace Carlos, just as he had for his international debut against Brazil. Argentina were winning 2–1 but manager Diego Maradona wanted more goals.

'Their defence is tired,' Maradona told Sergio. 'Get the ball and run at them!'

Sergio nodded – that was what he did best. A minute later, he passed to Lionel who ran past the defence and set up a goal for Gonzalo. Three minutes later, Lionel played a quick free-kick to Sergio and he ran forward. He passed to Gonzalo, who passed to Lionel, who passed it back to Sergio on the left. He chipped a great ball across to Gonzalo and he headed into the net for his hat-trick.

'What a great goal!' Lionel said as the three of them celebrated together. Sergio looked up into the crowd and saw a sea of Argentina flags. He loved playing for his country.

'Well done – Maradona won't leave you on the bench again!' Leo told him afterwards. He was so proud of the way his son had changed the game.

Sergio hoped that he had done enough to join Lionel and Gonzalo in Argentina's attacking trio. The team was improving with each game they played. Sergio started the final group game against Greece but he couldn't get a goal. As soon as he came off,

Argentina scored. Sergio was pleased for the team but he feared that his World Cup might be over.

'That was my big chance,' he told Lionel in the dressing room. 'Maradona will pick Gonzalo and Carlos for the next round.'

'Don't give up yet,' Lionel said, trying to cheer his friend up. 'When we beat Mexico there'll be another match!'

Argentina did beat Mexico in the knockout stage and Carlos and Gonzalo got the goals. The team next faced Germany in Cape Town. 'Hopefully I can come off the bench against Germany and score,' Sergio told his dad as he tried to stay positive.

But when Sergio came on, Argentina were three goals down, with Germany about to score a fourth. There was nothing he could do to rescue his country.

'We'll be back in four years,' Ángel said as they left the pitch in shock. 'And next time we'll win.'

Sergio had enjoyed his first World Cup experience but he went home very disappointed. 'Sorry and thanks,' Sergio wrote to the Argentina fans on social media. He didn't even watch the rest of the tournament; he was too upset. After a few weeks of sadness, Sergio returned to Spain with a new determination: 'It's time for me to show that I'm one of the best goalscorers in the world.'

CHAPTER 21

MOVING ON

Sergio raced towards the goal with the Mallorca defenders chasing him. The angle was very tight but if anyone could score, it was Sergio. In this last game of the 2010–11 Spanish season, he was enjoying his new role as Atlético Madrid captain.

In the second half, he controlled a high ball perfectly. Two defenders stood between him and the goal but Sergio could see that the goalkeeper was off his line. He quickly chipped the ball into the top corner. The Mallorca players couldn't believe what had happened.

'You made that look so easy!' his teammate Juanfran said. Sergio was still getting better and better. Yet he had still never scored a hat-trick for Atlético.

With ten minutes to go, Sergio got the ball on the left. There were defenders all around him but he wanted that third goal. He kicked it into the penalty area and ran on to it. Sergio knew he was the quickest player on the pitch. He lifted the ball over the diving goalkeeper and then passed it calmly into the net.

'Even six players can't stop you!' Juanfran shouted as he jumped on the hat-trick hero.

Sergio smiled; it was a nice way to end his time at Atlético Madrid. Twenty-seven goals in just forty-one games was the best season of his career but Sergio wanted a new challenge.

'I've been here for four years now,' he told the manager Quique Sánchez Flores. 'I've learnt so much and I love this club but I want to win more trophies.'

Atlético agreed to let him go if a club would pay £38 million. The fans were very unhappy to lose another superstar. How would they replace a striker who had scored over one hundred goals?

For Sergio, the big question was which clubs wanted to sign him? The media talked about Real Madrid, Chelsea, Juventus and Manchester City. He would be very happy to stay in Spain but a move to the Premier League would also be very interesting.

'I've watched English football for years,' he discussed with his dad. 'It's the most exciting league in the world. Do you remember when we used to watch Michael Owen and Steven Gerrard playing for Liverpool?'

'Michael Owen was your hero!' Leo said with a smile. 'The style is more physical than La Liga but you're strong enough to do well.'

The Manchester City manager, Roberto Mancini, invited Sergio to his house. 'Welcome to England!' Mancini said, shaking his hand. 'I'm sure you know about the big project we've started here. We need a world-class striker to help us win the Premiership and you're the one we want.'

Sergio was very impressed by Mancini's ambition. As he tried to make his decision, he called a good friend for some advice.

'Hi Kun!' Pablo Zabaleta said when he answered the phone. 'I hear you'll be joining me at Manchester City!'

Sergio laughed. He did like the idea of playing with his Argentinian teammate. It would really help him to settle into life in a new country.

'We've got a good team but we're missing some star quality in attack,' Pablo told him. 'With you and Carlos up front, we'll win the league!'

Sergio also spoke to Maxi, his old Atlético Madrid teammate who was now playing for Liverpool. 'You'll love the Premier League!' Maxi told him.

Sergio had made up his mind; he would join Manchester City. In the Number 16 shirt, he was ready to take England by storm.

'I'm here to win important trophies,' he told the media with lots of confidence. The Manchester City fans loved their new record signing and were already wearing his name on their shirts.

Sergio moved into a house near Pablo's and started having English lessons every week. Sergio found that life was much quieter in Manchester and he liked that. When he wasn't playing matches or training at the brilliant Etihad Campus, he relaxed at home. He got on really well with his new teammates too.

'Here comes our new thirty-goal striker!' captain Vincent Kompany joked. He would soon learn that Sergio loved this kind of pressure.

In August 2011, Sergio watched from the bench as City played local rivals Manchester United in the Community Shield. His team lost 3–2 but the passion of the fans was incredible. They sat much closer to the pitch in England and that created a brilliant atmosphere.

'That was even better than the Madrid derby!' Sergio said to Pablo.

'You wait until we play them in the league!' Pablo replied. He couldn't wait to get revenge.

Soon afterwards, in Manchester City's first league game of the new season, against Swansea City, Sergio came on with half an hour to go. On his back, he had asked for his nickname and his surname – 'KUN AGÜERO'. He couldn't wait to show the fans what he could do. City were 1–0 up but Mancini wanted another goal.

As he ran onto the pitch, the fans cheered loudly. Sergio knew it was going to be a good day. His first shots were saved but he kept going. He wanted a goal on his debut. Adam Johnson passed to Micah Richards on the right wing. Micah looked up and played the ball into the box. The Swansea defenders missed it and Sergio was there at the back post for a tap-in. It was a classic striker's goal.

'I'll score better ones, I promise!' he joked.

David Silva was the first to hug him. 'A goal is a goal – the fans don't care how beautiful they are!'

A few minutes later, Sergio chased down a defensive mistake, flicked the ball over the goalkeeper and then volleyed it back for David to score. In injury time, Sergio finished off a brilliant debut with another goal and it was one that he was very proud of. From twenty-five yards out, he hit a powerful shot into the top corner.

'I think £38 million's a bargain!' Micah said with a big smile.

hours but the next day, the team focused again on their ultimate target.

'We want to be top of the league at Christmas,' Mancini told his players. Thanks to two more goals from Sergio against Stoke on 21 December, City achieved that. Sergio was also named on the shortlist for the Ballon D'Or award. Lionel was the favourite to win that prize but even so, Sergio was very proud to be one of the twenty best players in the world.

'United are always better in the second half of the season,' Vincent reminded the squad. 'We have to keep winning!'

By the start of April 2012, United had replaced City at the top of the league. After such a brilliant start, Sergio was struggling to find form.

'We keep losing 1–0,' he complained to his dad. 'We need goals and I'm supposed to be our main goalscorer.'

'Kun, I know you like playing under pressure but take it easy,' Leo said. 'If you play your natural game, the goals will come.'

A home match against West Brom was the perfect

'Wow!' Mancini said at the final whistle, putting an arm around his shoulders. 'If you play that well when you're coming back from injury, what can you do when you're 100 per cent fit?!'

Sergio was very tired but very pleased. He had worked very hard for the team. The City fans would now expect amazing things from him in every game. Sergio would do everything he could to not disappoint them.

CHAPTER 22

PREMIER LEAGUE WINNER

Sergio loved playing for City. With talented
midfielders like David Silva, Yaya Touré and Samir
Nasri, he had lots of chances to score. Against
Wigan, David set up his first goal and Samir set
up his second. Then David played a brilliant pass
behind the defence. Sergio was through on goal
and he calmly shot past the goalkeeper. He had
a hat-trick and it was only his fourth Premier
League match.

'Do you ever miss?' David joked.

'You guys make my life very easy!' Sergio replied.

Sometimes players took a few months to get used
to English football but not Sergio. He was born to

play in the Premiership. He was quick, strong, ski
and brilliant at shooting. The City fans loved him
straight away.

Agüero! Agüero! Agüero!

By October 2011, after eight games, City were
of the league. Their next match was a very impor
game against the team in second place: Manches
United.

'If you score today, you'll be a City legend!' Pa
shouted to him in the tunnel at Old Trafford. Th
noise in the stadium was incredible. Sergio woul
never forget that day.

City played brilliantly and Mario Balotelli sco
twice. 'United are all over the place – let's scor
more goals!' he said as they celebrated. Sergio
desperate to get on the scoresheet.

Micah ran down the right wing. He knew
where Sergio would be and his cross was per
Sergio was so happy with his goal and the ga
finished 6–1 to City.

'That's our greatest ever win!' Vincent sa
dressing room afterwards. The party went

time for Sergio to find the net again. 'Be patient and take the chances when they come,' was Mancini's advice before kick-off.

Six minutes into the game, the first chance came. Samir passed to him and Sergio ran forward at full speed. A defender tried to tackle him but he shrugged him off. As he got close to the penalty area, Sergio slowed down and prepared to shoot. He was desperate to score. He kicked the ball with lots of power and it swerved through the air and under the goalkeeper's arm.

'That's the Kun we know and love!' Vincent shouted as they celebrated with the fans behind the goal.

Sergio scored another goal in the West Brom game, then two against Norwich and one against Wolves. Suddenly, the City fans believed their team could still win the league – but the players had never stopped believing.

'We have three games left,' Mancini told them. 'If we win all three, we will be champions.'

The first of those games was the second

Manchester derby. The atmosphere was very tense at the Etihad Stadium because neither team wanted to make a big mistake. Sergio had a couple of very good chances but he couldn't score. Thankfully, Vincent scored a header to give them a 1–0 win.

'Two games left,' Mancini told them afterwards. 'If we win both, we will be champions.'

Sergio had scored twenty-nine goals in all competitions and he was nominated for both the PFA Player of the Year and Young Player of the Year awards. He was very proud of himself but he was determined to win the title to make it a perfect first Premier League season. He set up Yaya Touré's first goal in a 2–0 win against Newcastle. The race would go down to the last day. City were at home to QPR and United were away at Sunderland.

'We have played so well this season,' Vincent said. 'All we need is one more win!'

Sergio had signed for Manchester City to star in big matches like this. They hadn't won the league in forty-four years. He knew he needed to be the hero. He was ready for the responsibility.

After going 1–0 up, City were losing 2–1 with a few minutes left. Meanwhile, Manchester United were beating Sunderland and would win the league unless Sergio and his teammates could score two more goals. The City fans were starting to give up on their dream.

'We can still do this!' Vincent screamed and Sergio really believed it, especially when Edin Džeko scored a header to make it 2–2. He was having a bad game but no-one could score late winning goals like Sergio. He remained as calm as ever, and in the last minute of injury time, and with the support of Mario, scored a thrilling winning goal. It was the greatest feeling in the world.

It was the most exciting end to a Premier League season ever. After a forty-four-year gap, Manchester City were finally the Champions of England again and Sergio was their hero. It was the best night of his life, and the perfect end to the best season of his career.

CHAPTER 23

HUNGRY
FOR MORE

Sergio couldn't wait for the new season of 2012–13 to start. 'I want to win the Premier League again,' he told Vincent Kompany and David Silva in pre-season training, 'and I want to win the Champions League too!'

Early in the first match against Southampton, Nathaniel Clyne slid in for a tackle on Sergio. It wasn't a bad foul but Sergio's right leg twisted at a bad angle. As he fell to the ground, Sergio knew it was serious.

'Ow!' he screamed, holding his knee. There was no way that he could stand up, let alone play on. The physio ran onto the pitch, took a quick look at the injury and told Mancini to get a substitute ready.

Sergio was really upset. After years of playing so much football, he found it very difficult to sit still and watch his teammates instead. In his first season at City, he had only missed a few games due to injury.

'What if I can't play for months?' he asked his dad. That would be a nightmare. 'What will I do?'

'The only thing you can do is rest and then work hard to get back to full fitness,' Leo replied.

The good news was that the knee injury wasn't as bad as they had feared. The bad news was that Sergio would still have to go a month without playing football. To pass the time, he watched NFL games at home with Pablo.

'Their acceleration is so good,' Sergio said excitedly. 'They must have really strong legs to move so quickly and get away from the tackles.'

'Sounds like someone else I know!' Pablo joked. He loved the way that Sergio was always looking to improve his game. He never stopped learning new tricks.

'I'm counting down the days until I'm back on the pitch!' Sergio told Mancini. 'I can't wait to win back my starting spot.'

Mancini loved his superstar's passion but he was worried. 'Kun, we need to look after you carefully. We have a lot of important matches this season but you won't be able to play in every single one.'

Sergio was disappointed but he understood what his manager was saying. City needed him to stay fit and healthy, and sometimes that would mean resting or being a substitute.

'If you feel any pain at all, you have to tell us and come off,' Mancini told him.

It was a tough season for Sergio, and City finished second behind Manchester United. Every time he started to score lots of goals again, Sergio picked up another injury. None of them were serious but they slowed down his progress. Seventeen goals was good for most strikers but Sergio wasn't 'most strikers'.

'I got thirty goals last season,' he reminded Pablo. 'Seventeen is only just over half of that!'

'Kun, you're still our top striker!' Pablo said. 'Next season, you'll be back to your brilliant best.'

Sergio worked really hard over the summer of 2013 to make sure that was true. In the first match of the next season, against Newcastle, Manchester City were brilliant. David, Edin and Sergio were unstoppable in attack and City could have scored at least ten times. Edin flicked the ball through to Sergio and he ran towards goal. The defender pushed him wide towards the right but Sergio didn't mind. He could shoot from any angle. As he reached the edge of the penalty area, he placed a perfect finish into the bottom corner.

'That's the first of many!' David laughed. City were off to a great start.

A few weeks later, it was time for another Manchester derby. Sergio couldn't wait to beat their biggest rivals again. He still loved playing football just as much as when he was a young boy. Last season he had scored the winner at Old Trafford. Every time he scored against United, the fans loved him a little bit more.

Samir passed to Aleksandar Kolarov on the left and he crossed into the penalty area. The ball was behind

Sergio but he hooked a brilliant volley into the top corner. It was a moment of magic and the Etihad Stadium went wild.

'What a goal!' Vincent shouted over the noise of the fans. 'How did you do that?'

Sergio just shrugged. It was natural talent.

At the start of the second half, Álvaro Negredo battled for the ball. When he won it, he knew exactly where his strike partner would be. Sergio arrived in the six-yard box just in time to put the ball in the net.

'Thanks Álvaro!' Sergio said as they celebrated. They were forming another great partnership.

Everything was going so well for City and Sergio scored another wonderful volley against Arsenal. However, in the second half, Sergio played a one-two with David and felt a sharp pain in his calf. He tried to run it off but he couldn't. He lay down on the grass with his head in his hands. The physios looked worried as they carried him off the pitch, and so did the supporters. They could be without their number-one superstar for a while.

'Not another injury!' Sergio said to himself. He couldn't believe it. He would miss the busy Christmas schedule but his team just kept on winning.

'You don't even need me!' he told Pablo. He was half joking but it was difficult to watch them play so well without him. The team was improving all the time but he missed being part of it.

Sergio would return and would score some more great goals but then he injured his hamstring. He was only twenty-five but his body was starting to feel very old. He needed to look after himself and not rush back to the team when he was only 75 per cent fit. He worked hard in the gym and he improved his diet, eating as many vegetables as possible.

'Don't worry, Kun,' City's new manager Manuel Pellegrini said, trying to cheer him up. 'You'll be back just in time for the League Cup final!'

City had made it all the way to Wembley and Sergio was desperate to be fit enough to play against Sunderland. He was so happy when he was named in the starting line-up.

'Come on boys, I want another winner's medal!' he told his teammates in the dressing room. It was another important match and another chance to shine on the big stage.

Sergio tried and tried to score but he wasn't feeling 100 per cent. He wasn't as fast as he normally was and his skills weren't working. Luckily, Yaya and Samir saved the day and City won the cup. At the final whistle, Sergio ran from the substitutes' bench to celebrate with the others.

'We couldn't have done it without you!' Vincent told him as they went up to collect the trophy. Sergio loved his teammates and he loved the club. It really felt like home.

'Now we've got a league to go and win!' Sergio reminded everyone. Liverpool played really well and the title race went down to the final game again. If Manchester City could beat West Ham, they would be champions again.

'Let's hope we don't need some magic from you this time!' Pablo joked as they prepared for the big game.

'I'll be ready just in case!' Sergio replied. He had lots of faith in the team but he was born to be a hero. In the Premier League, he had scored seventeen goals in only twenty-three games.

City won 2–0 for a second Premier League title in three years. Making the brave move to Manchester was the best thing Sergio had ever done. It was so nice to have Leo and Adriana there to celebrate with him. Thanks to their love and support, Sergio had risen from poverty in Argentina to become a double winner of the best league in the world. It had been an amazing journey and Sergio was thankful to everyone who had helped him along the way.

Thousands of City fans ran on to the pitch to share the success with the players. There was a blue-and-white party in Manchester that night and Sergio loved every minute of it. As soon as it was over, however, Sergio was thinking ahead. He was never satisfied and that's what made him so special.

'Winning two Premier League titles is great but now we need to win the Champions League!'

SERGIO AGÜERO HONOURS

Atlético Madrid
* ★ UEFA Intertoto Cup: 2007
* ★ UEFA Europa League: 2009–10
* ★ UEFA Super Cup: 2010

Manchester City
* ★ Premier League: 2011–12, 2013–14
* ★ FA Community Shield: 2012
* ★ Football League Cup: 2013–14, 2015–16

Argentina
* ★ FIFA Under-20 World Cup: 2005, 2007
* ★ Olympic Gold Medal: 2008

Individual

★ FIFA Young Player of the Year: 2007

★ FIFA Under-20 World Cup Golden Shoe: 2007

★ FIFA Under-20 World Cup Golden Ball: 2007

★ Don Balón Award: 2007–08

★ La Liga Ibero-American Player of the Year: 2008

★ World Soccer Young Player of the Year: 2009

★ Etihad Player of the Year: 2011–12, 2014–15

★ Etihad Goal of the Season: 2011–12

★ Football Supporters' Federation Player of the Year: 2014

★ Premier League Golden Boot: 2014–15

★ Premier League Player of the Month: October 2013, November 2014, January 2016, April 2016

Turn the page for a sneak preview of
another brilliant football story by
Matt and Tom Oldfield. . .

RAHEEM STERLING
YOUNG LION

Available now!

978 1 78418 646 3

A DREAM
COME TRUE

This was the biggest day of Raheem's life so far —
after all, you only made your England debut once.
Two months earlier, he had been called up for the
World Cup 2014 qualifier against Ukraine and
named as a substitute. He didn't get to come on but
he learned a lot from training with the country's
best players. It was hard watching from the bench,
especially when the team was losing with ten
minutes to go. With his pace and skill, Raheem knew
he could have made a difference on the wing against
a tired defence but in the end, England managed to
get a draw without him.

This time, in Sweden, not only was Raheem

playing but he was starting. 'I'll be testing some of
the younger players in tomorrow's friendly,' Roy
Hodgson, the England manager, had told him as
they walked off the training pitch the day before.
'You'll be starting, Raheem – we believe you're
ready for this.' Roy had always had great faith in
him; at Liverpool, he had given him his debut at
the age of just 15. Raheem could only nod and flash
his trademark big smile. It was the news he'd been
waiting for.

In the tunnel before the match, he took a deep
breath and let the noise of the 50,000 fans in the
stadium fire him up. This was what he was born to
do. Moments later, he walked out onto the pitch in
Stockholm, holding the hand of a Swedish mascot.
Just like at Liverpool, Steven Gerrard was there
with him as captain and mentor. In the dressing
room before the game, Stevie could see that Raheem
was nervous.

'There's nothing to worry about, kid. It's no
different to playing in front of the Kop at Liverpool.
Don't rush things today - just do your thing and

enjoy it. Something tells me this won't be your only England cap!'

Stevie patted him on the back and left him to his pre-match stretches. It was a real comfort to have such experienced teammates alongside him – these big games could be pretty scary for a 17-year-old.

As the national anthem played, Raheem looked down proudly at the famous three lions on his white tracksuit top. He still couldn't quite believe that he was wearing the England shirt so soon into his career. What a year 2012 had been and there was still a month to go. Despite being born in Jamaica, England was certainly Raheem's footballing home. His homeland would always have a special place in his heart but it was in London and Liverpool that he had developed as both a player and a person.

Just before kick-off, another Liverpool teammate, Glen Johnson, came over to give him some words of advice. 'Raheem, stay focused today. You're on the right wing and I'm at right back so we'll be working together a lot. Make those amazing attacking runs when you can but don't forget to defend too. I don't want to spend the whole game clearing up your mess!' Glen gave him a friendly slap on the back and they took up their positions ready for the start.

Raheem knew it wouldn't be an easy game; Sweden had experienced Premier League players like Jonas Olsson and Seb Larsson, plus one of his favourite players in the world, the amazing striker Zlatan Ibrahimovic. Raheem was really looking forward to playing against Zlatan and seeing his tricks and flicks up close. Zlatan did not disappoint, scoring the first goal after 20 minutes.

Five minutes later, Raheem found space for the first time in the match and he ran at the Swedish defence before passing to Danny Welbeck, who nearly set up a goal. Raheem could sense the Sweden fans holding their breath when he had the ball at his feet. They knew he was a threat and that gave him confidence.

Raheem was involved again as England made it 1-1. Stevie passed to him deep inside his own half and this time, rather than dribbling, he did what coaches had always told him to do – 'get your head up and look up for the pass'. He could see Ashley

Young making a great run over on the left and he played a great ball out to him. Ashley did brilliantly and crossed for Danny to score.

England took the lead before half-time but the second half was all about Zlatan. His second goal was a volley, his third was a powerful free-kick and his fourth was one of the best goals Raheem had ever seen, an impossible overhead kick from 30 yards out. Watching such an amazing performance, Raheem was sure that he had the desire and the talent to be that good. He just needed to keep working hard.

With five minutes to go, Raheem was substituted. 'Well done, lad,' Roy said as he made his way off the pitch. As he took his seat on the bench, Raheem felt really tired but pleased with the way he had played. It hadn't been the dream debut he had hoped for but it had been an amazing experience to represent his country. He couldn't wait to do it again, especially back at Wembley. As a kid, he had lived around the corner from the new stadium, playing football in the streets as it was being built. To play on that pitch in front of all those fans would be unbelievable.

On the flight back to England, Raheem thought back on how far he'd come. There were times when his future had looked bleak. But thanks to football, he stayed out of trouble and learnt respect, hard work and self-esteem. He owed a lot of people for the support they had given him over the years – his mum Nadine, his teachers, his coaches. They had all believed in his talent.

Most of all, he thought about what Chris, his teacher at Vernon House, had once said to him. 'If you carry on the way you're going, by the time you're 17 you'll either be in prison or playing for England.' Raheem smiled to himself; thankfully, he had achieved the second option. But he promised himself that this was just the beginning.

COLLECT THEM ALL

STEVEN GERRARD CAPTAIN FANTASTIC

ZLATAN IBRAHIMOVIĆ RED DEVIL

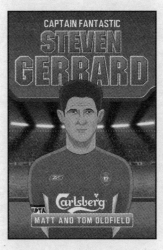

Steven Gerrard: Captain Fantastic tells of how a young boy from Merseyside overcame personal tragedy in the Hillsborough disaster to make his dream of playing for Liverpool FC come true. But that boy was no ordinary footballer; he would go on to captain his club for over a decade, inspiring their legendary Champions League FA Cup wins along the way. This is the story of Steven Gerrard, Liverpool's greatest ever player.

978 1 78606 219 2
£5.99

Zlatan Ibrahimović: Red Devil follows the Swedish superstar on his amazing journey from the tough streets of Malmö to becoming the deadly striker at Manchester United. Along the way he has been a star for Juventus, Inter Milan, Barcelona, and Paris Saint-Germain, as well as becoming Sweden's all-time leading goal scorer. This is the story of one of a generation's finest footballers.

978 1 78606 217 8
£5.99

COLLECT THEM ALL

ALEXIS SÁNCHEZ
THE WONDER BOY

LUIS SUAREZ
EL PISTOLERO

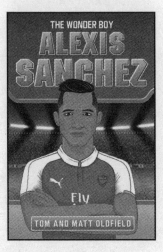

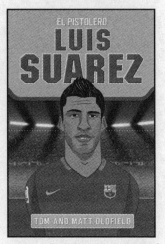

Alexis Sánchez: The Wonder Boy tells the story of the Arsenal superstar's incredible journey from the streets of Tocopilla to become 'The Boy Wonder', a national hero, and one of the most talented players in the world. With his pace, skill and eye for a goal, Alexis is now one of the Premier League's biggest stars. The story is every bit as exciting as the player.

978 1 78606 013 6
£5.99

Luis Suárez: El Pistolero follows the Uruguayan's winding path from love-struck youngster to Liverpool hero to Barcelona star. Grabbing goals and headlines along the way, Luis chased his dreams and became a Champions League winner. This is the inspiring story of how the world's deadliest striker made his mark.

978 1 786060129
£5.99

COLLECT THEM ALL

EDEN HAZARD
THE BOY IN BLUE

GARETH BALE
THE BOY WHO BECAME
A GALÁCTICO

Eden Hazard: The Boy in Blue is the thrilling tale of how the wing wizard went from local wonder kid to league champion. With the support of his football-obsessed family, Eden worked hard to develop his amazing dribbling skills and earn his dream transfer to Chelsea.

978 1 78606 014 3
£5.99

Gareth Bale: The Boy Who Became a Galáctico tracks the Welsh wizard's impressive rise from talented schoolboy to Real Madrid star. This is the inspiring story of how Bale beat the odds and became the most expensive player in football history.

978 1 78418 645 7
£5.99

COLLECT THEM ALL

WAYNE ROONEY
CAPTAIN OF ENGLAND

RAHEEM STERLING
YOUNG LION

Wayne Rooney: Captain of England tells the action-packed story of one boy's journey from the streets of Croxteth to one of the biggest stages in world football. This heartwarming book tracks Rooney's fairytale rise from child superstar to Everton hero to Manchester United legend.

978 1 78418 647 0
£5.99

Raheem Sterling: Young Lion is the exciting tale of a boy who followed his passion and became one of the most dynamic young players in world football, winning the hearts of Liverpool and England fans along the way. Relive Sterling's whirlwind journey in this uplifting story.

978 1 78418 646 3
£5.99